HAROLD GIMBLETT

Tormented Genius of Cricket

HAROLD GIMBLETT

Tormented Genius of Cricket

David Foot

To Alan
Best wishes
— David Foot

HEINEMANN : LONDON

*To Anne; to Mark and Vivien; to Julia; to my parents;
to my timeless heroes of Somerset cricket.
With love.*

William Heinemann Ltd
10 Upper Grosvenor Street, London W1X 9PA
LONDON   MELBOURNE   TORONTO
JOHANNESBURG   AUCKLAND

First published 1982
Reprinted 1983
© David Foot 1982
SBN 434 26820 8

Printed and bound in Great Britain by
Butler & Tanner Limited, Frome & London

CONTENTS

ILLUSTRATIONS

ACKNOWLEDGEMENTS

My thanks must go primarily, because of the nature of this book, to Harold Gimblett himself because he trusted me enough to leave some exceedingly personal tapes, containing his most intimate and painful thoughts, to my discretion. His widow, Marguerita, has been helpful and cooperative at all times; never less than honest in trying to explain the vicissitudes of the man she knew better than anyone else. I am grateful, too, to Harold's brother, the Rev Dennis Gimblett, who from his home in Australia sent me the kind of assessment that was equally valuable.

It was in many ways a cumulative portrait on my part. I have talked to many cricketers over many years about him. In particular, I am grateful to Bill Andrews, Horace Hazell, Eric Hill, Micky Walford, Ben Brocklehurst, the late Frank Lee and Les Angell. For impressions of West Buckland school days, I went to Harold Boyer; for, more specifically, the strong links with West Somerset, I talked to kindly and wise souls like Bromley Penny, whose father (the other WG) was Gimblett's mentor, and journalist Jack Hurley.

Cricket historian Keith Ball researched with unfailing good humour and diligence. Ronald Priddle told me about Harold's years in the Fire Service, while the Rev Derek Chapman remembered the cricketer's final days at Verwood. Dr Ken Smith helped to interpret for me some of the inner battles that Harold was fighting. Hampshire scorer Vic Isaacs also provided me with an elusive fact or two; likewise, Somerset's meticulous statistician, Michael Hill.

I thank George Baker, an erstwhile sports editor of mine for the loan of pictures; others kindly came from Bill Andrews, the *Bristol Evening Post*, Mrs Gimblett, Roy Dight – a family friend of Harold who also showed me some private correspondence – and my son Mark. My thanks go to Alan Gibson, for allowing me to quote freely from his address at the memorial service.

Harold had a warm regard for John Arlott and it was appropriate to ask him to write the Foreword; I thank him for the generosity of his comments. The writing of the book involved some unavoidable prying on my part. It was both a rewarding and harrowing experience, listening again to Harold's voice; and if, as I suspect, I was affected by the moods of my subject, I should be all the more grateful for the tolerance of my wife.

FOREWORD
by John Arlott

There has never been a cricket book quite like this 'life of a great batsman in torment'. David Foot has written it with compassion, something not far from passion, and sympathy, out of a childhood admiration. It is a remarkable achievement that, in spite of those emotive factors, he has maintained an admirable objectivity.

It is not a biography, nor an autobiography, nor the data for a psychological study; but something of all three. Harold Gimblett made some very revealing tapes for a book of his views on cricket, which he hoped Mr Foot might write for him. He had not dictated enough for that purpose when he died, but his own words serve as completely effective illustrations of the author's points in what is, in many ways, a study of a state of mind.

As one who witnessed many of the phases of this story – including ducking under a thrown bat in that gloomy old pros' dressing room at Taunton – it is possible to say that, at every point where it is possible to check from personal knowledge, it is completely accurate. This is the story of a life which, within the small world of cricket, ascended to the heights: but, at the level where life is truly lived, plumbed the ultimate depth.

Such books are rarely written about games players; certainly not about cricketers. Perhaps their mental problems are not regarded as sufficiently complex to interest a literate public.

Stories roughly comparable in setting, playing success against living failure, might have been provided by A. E. Stoddart, Albert Trott, Arthur Shrewsbury and Percy Chapman. No one, though, had any such pure first-hand evidence on them as Harold Gimblett's tapes; nor came to write while testimony of contemporaries and intimates was still plentifully available. David Frith, in his admirable study of Stoddart, lacked those two advantages: and no one has attempted to write seriously of the others; in one case, at least, because the relevant documents were destroyed.

There were few sadder dual experiences in cricket than being exhilarated by a sustained innings in which Harold Gimblett went on and on treating good bowling with almost Jove-like contempt; and, afterwards, going in, hoping to make a small contribution of admiration to a moment of glory, only for all those with the same purpose – friends, fellow players, even relations – to meet a remark – not aimed at them but at that world which he felt he owed a grudge – of such bitterness as marred the former splendour. It was better not to go; but to bask in the recollection of the performance and attempt to treat it impersonally. That was not possible because Harold Gimblett's cricket was personal: and because he compelled affection. The sheer anger of a batsman out through what he construes as stupid error or ill-luck is understandable. Lack of pleasure in a great innings – and many of Harold Gimblett's were great in their attacking qualities – is the very negation of cricket emotions. That is the measure of his affliction and his deprivation: and why he prompted a protective urge.

Yet this was the man who once, in a Bournemouth hotel, joined in a skylarking soda-water syphon battle with all the high-spirited abandon of a schoolboy; and, oddly enough, recalled it from time to time, for years afterwards with such mirth as to laugh himself to tears.

Mr Foot is sound in his references to Rita Gimblett: Harold's life must have been more agonized and, probably, shorter but for his wife's calm, and unfailingly considerate, presence; as gentle as she looked, she had in her, too, all her days, a vein of the pure innocence which Harold strove, against his unhappiest urges, never to injure.

It is doubtful if cricket will see such a book again. Fortunately the game has few such subjects. If there were more, it would be all too easy to sensationalize the story, or 'smear' the man, by failure to understand. Few would devote so much time and trouble to research as Mr Foot has done – not heavy-handedly, but in making contact with the right witnesses; and in uncovering balancing, and counter-balancing, evidence. Those who knew Harold Gimblett can shed a not unworthy tear into this book; those who did not, will find themselves moved by a story the more affecting for being recorded with such dignity.

From the great days; through the ironic – indeed, almost comic – episode of that infernal carbuncle – to the crippled, groping giant of the Verwood days, tragedy was never far from Harold Gimblett's elbow. At times it was as if his fellows in the Somerset dressing room sensed its presence. Surely there was a measure of that in the fact that he was never given a nickname, was always 'Harold'. Someone tried once – during the Civil Defence days, when he had just come in after a fast and entertaining sixty. 'Come on, Corkscrew,' he said, 'why don't you give us a big laugh.' 'I haven't got anything to laugh about,' was the reply; and, as David Foot shows, with such perception, that was the truth.

THE INTRODUCTION

Harold Gimblett is the greatest batsman Somerset has ever produced.

He wiped the mud off his farm boots and as part of a West Country romance, quoted more graphically and affectionately than Exmoor's own Lorna Doone, he hitched a lift to Frome before scoring a sensationally fast and fearless century on his county debut. No one has yet scored more runs, hit more hundreds or reached a higher score (310 at Eastbourne) for Somerset.

Gimblett has no native rival and my lofty assessment cannot readily be challenged. Lionel Palairet came from Lancashire and Ian Botham from Cheshire, Sammy Woods from Australia and Vivian Richards from Antigua. Harold Gimblett was born in a creeper-clad Bicknoller farmhouse, on the other side of the Quantocks from the county ground in Taunton. This undulating, red-earthed corner of West Somerset also nurtured J. C. White. The home of Bill Greswell, one of the innovators of late inswing bowling and subsequently the county president, was only a few boundary lengths away. Those rolling hills had the tang of freshly cut grass and linseed oil.

In a county renowned for the muscle and imprudence of its batsmen, Gimblett could be the most audacious of them all. Very few opening batsmen have hit more steepling sixes, have so

1

readily dismissed caution in the first over of the day, delighted more schoolboys or threatened more diehards, shorn of imagination, with apoplexy. He played for Somerset from 1935 till 1954 and cattle market trade, across the road from the cosy county ground, fluctuated according to Gimblett's prowess at the wicket: the farmers left the pens and put their cheque books away when he was in full flow. On early closing day in Taunton, the cricket attendance depended on him. Hundreds of fresh-faced boys also put radio sets surreptitiously to their ears to discover whether he was still in and therefore whether a sprint to St James Street after last period was worth it.

Marguerita (Rita) Gimblett told me: 'I was just as bad. I used to find out from the radio whether Harold was going well. If he was, I'd rush along to the ground. Sometimes, by the time I got there, the spectators would be streaming away, glum and silent. And I always knew what that meant – he was out!'

He played just three times for England and not only Somerset's cricket lovers, who doted on his deeds, were aggrieved. Some would argue that he contributed to that kind of wanton neglect by a defensive, tetchy manner that found less than favour with the game's hierarchy including Sir Pelham Warner. Gimblett was never servile or particularly tactful; his withering observations, not always out of earshot, could easily be misconstrued. Some of his verbal strokes had every bit as much venom as those that scorched past extra cover. It should also be remembered, to adjust the perspective, that in the post-war years, Hutton and Washbrook were two other valid reasons for his scant recognition as a Test player.

Harold Gimblett was a marvellous cricketer by so many standards. At times, his batting, instinctively classical when the mood was right – and more exhilarating than any of his contemporaries – came near to genius. The farmer's boy diligently improved his defence, learned how to hook, from one of his great idols, Herbert Sutcliffe and became a stylist who could fashion his innings as handsomely as Palairet once did. His cover drive was even envied by Hammond, though the pair had no natural

2

rapport; the straight drive for six, a mischief maker off the first ball of the innings, was flawless in its ruthless execution.

I first saw him play during the Thirties in my home town of Yeovil. It was an annual fixture for Somerset, and Gimblett was the attraction, along with Wellard who was expected to put balls out of sight over the Westland hangers, and Andrews who used to cut the grass and coach the local boys for the squire at thirty bob a week at nearby East Coker.

This Gimblett, I remembered, had broad shoulders, boyish good looks and an extraordinary under-arm throw from the outfield that left careless batsmen stranded in mid wicket. In those same early days he bowled gentle seamers and occasional off breaks; they brought him a few wickets, too, but I was never around to see them.

At this point I should perhaps declare an interest. Gimblett was my hero; and so he was of every other West Country boy who believed cricket was the best game God ever invented. But schoolboys can be conveniently selective in their idolatry: it does not usually extend beyond the scorecard. It is based on wondrous innings and tales of outrageous aggression that are exaggerated each time in the telling. We accepted without question that Harold Gimblett ritualistically converted every opening delivery into a half-volley; that he tamed a tiring Larwood, mastered the fiery Nichols and Farnes; that he despatched Miller and Lindwall with disdain; that he was the man to put Ramadhin and Valentine in their place.

Hero worship is healthy; but such doting dreams are fragile. Harold in the flesh, as I discovered some years later, was not always an engaging person. Once during a county match at Street, he stalked to the press tent and rounded on an erstwhile colleague of mine, A. C. H. Smith, the Bristol writer, because he had dared to criticize in print the state of the wicket at Millfield where at that time Gimblett was employed. The reprimand was public and condescending and it took some years before I privately forgave him.

This book is not a homage. The forthright Gimblett would

3

have deprecated that. I hope it will help to show what a complex person he was and that his troubled mind, which eventually led him to suicide in March 1978, was largely responsible for his vicissitudes of mood, the brusque retorts and the overriding pessimism. There is also much evidence that he could be a man of considerable charm and kindness.

Two years before he died he phoned me one evening from his home, then at Minehead. Would I help him write a book? 'I don't want it to be like any of the other cricket books. I want the public to know what it is really like being a professional sportsman, when you're a worrier. The mental battles for me have been enormous and maybe it would be a good idea to put it on record.' I got the impression that he also saw the exercise as a form of therapy.

We had a long, relaxed conversation and I was concerned about the mounting phone bill. He laughed and said we were on the cheap rate. It was good to hear him laugh, something he had done less and less in recent years. I knew of his increasing anxieties about money matters – unnecessarily so – and I was reassured that he had deliberately chosen when he should ring me.

He told me he had bought a small cassette recorder and I encouraged him to start putting thoughts, as they occurred to him, down on tape. We talked again on the phone from time to time. 'I'm doing it in the middle of the night when I can't sleep . . . It's going to be very personal.' We agreed that when he felt he had said all he wanted to, we would have a meeting. He would let me have the various cassettes and I could use them as the basis for a book.

The meeting never took place. There were intermittent phone calls between us and he moved to Verwood. I waited for the summons. Then, with a ghastly suddenness, I read of his death.

I assumed that the cassettes, real or mythical, had in effect died with him. But several months later, a relative wrote to me to say they existed. At that point I did not know Mrs Gimblett and after a decent pause, I approached her rather diffidently. We began to meet; she was helpful and cooperative. With her, I returned to

Harold's birthplace at Bicknoller. We walked along the sylvan lanes where they used to do their courting.

At home I listened to the cassettes. They were like very private documents that he wanted now to make public. They were subjective: astute, perceptive, belligerent, unhappy and at times on the point of being irrational. Occasionally I found myself fidgeting in the way of a person caught eavesdropping. The moods were all there, elation and wretchedness. But his cricketing achievements, remembered with consistent modesty, seemed subordinate to other aspects of his life.

The final cassettes, heavy with despair and with Harold's voice trailing away into little pits of agonized reverie, contrasted sharply with his almost chirpy opening words:

> David, this is my attempt at a possible book. The only thing I'm absolutely certain of is the title. At the ripe old age of 62, I feel the title must be 'No More Bouncers' . . . not that I was ever afraid of 'em.

He took more than his share of bouncers, on and off the field. But this is a slightly different book and the title has been changed. Harold's brutally honest words were the starting point. I have honoured his wish not to make this simply a cricketing record. Rather have I tried to explain why he chose to be dismissive about his own vast talents and the game which gave him a living. He ended up with a contempt for cricket and I have attempted to untangle some of the complexes that caused this. It was apparently no great thrill for him to play for his country. By the end, as he leaned on his stick and hobbled along the Verwood country roads, he almost appeared to hate the game. He would cut short any conversation about it; sentimental allusions to his maiden century made him both embarrassed and angry. Harold had rejected cricket, the sport he adored with such dynamic and joyful panache.

Periodically through the book I quote him verbatim from the cassettes. Not all is gloom. There are shafts of bright sunshine.

There are illuminating encounters with great cricketing names. There are shrewd, considered judgements that show what an intelligent man he was.

It is a melancholy and not irrelevant fact that other fine cricketers, for a variety of reasons, have killed themselves.

William Scotton played for his country fifteen times between 1881–86. But by 1893 he had lost his place in the Nottinghamshire side and this, according to the inquest that followed his suicide, preyed seriously on his mind. Certainly his loss of form depressed him.

The magnificent Arthur Shrewsbury, immortalized by Dr Grace's sweeping compliment, shot himself one May evening in 1903, the season after he gave up playing for Nottinghamshire. Latterly he worried unnecessarily about an illness and pined for summers' days back at the wicket. Arthur played 23 times for England and was the outstanding professional of his day. Those glories no longer sustained him; he could not bear to think that his cricket was over for good.

Albert Trott played for both his native Australia and England. From 1898 he played for Middlesex and, it could be wryly claimed, he had indelible links with Somerset. He was given the Somerset fixture for his benefit match in 1907 and with exquisite timing he spectacularly demolished the West Country side's second innings. Trott started by taking the wickets of Lewis, Poyntz, Woods and Robson in four balls; then he finished off the innings with another hat-trick. In spite of such dramatics and some magnificent hitting, Trott was already on the wane and was no longer seen, arguably, as the best all-rounder in the world. He had suffered various rejections, like being left out of the ninth Australian side to tour England. His private proclivities were apparently a matter of some concern and there were innuendos about his liaisons with a Taunton woman of, as they quaintly said in those priggish, hypocritical days, 'easy virtue'. He was a great cricketer but by 1914, with war looming, he had had enough of life. He shot himself in his lonely London digs.

That was a year before A. E. Stoddart, of Middlesex and

England, who twice captained his country in Australia, shot himself through the head.

And then there was R. C. Robertson-Glasgow, who enjoyed his cricket like Gimblett for Somerset; and who, like him, died from an overdose of drugs. He was a lovable player who traded on gentle eccentricity and was apt to bamboozle various captains by disappearing into the beer tent at Bath and Weston between wickets. His felicitous prose also hummed with humour. His private pain he kept to himself.

Is it just a quirky coincidence that half a dozen especially talented cricketers – no doubt there are others – killed themselves? Certainly in most of those cases cricket, indirectly at least, was a contributory cause.

Like few other sports of the field, cricket is played very much with the mind. Only the unimaginative player escapes the tensions. Many, whatever their seeming unconcern, retreat into caverns of introspection. I long ago discovered that for the professional cricketers, particularly the sensitive ones, the match-winning cheers and bar-room bonhomie are outweighed by collective self-doubt and dressing room silences. Harold Gimblett knew all about that.

He had no more regard for cricket writers than he had for selectors and committee men. Robertson-Glasgow was the exception. Their playing careers hardly coincided at all. But Gimblett liked Crusoe's warm-hearted approach. They got on well together and the Oxford man's scholarship and double-barrelled name, and companionable nature, appealed to Gimblett. When Harold and Rita were on honeymoon in Torquay, idly looking in a dress shop window, a familiar voice bellowed across the street: 'Why don't you two get married?'

Sheepishly they looked up and recognized the affable enquirer. 'We've just done that very thing,' said Harold, to Crusoe's obvious surprise.

The regard was mutual. In one of his *Cricket Prints*, Robertson-Glasgow wrote of Gimblett: 'Someone remarked that perhaps he is too daring for the grey-beards. My own view is that he is also

7

too daring for the majority of the black-beards, the brown-beards and the all-beards, who sit in judgement on batsmen; in short, too daring for those who have never known what it is to dare in cricket . . .'

In this book I have tried to balance my own native affection for Gimblett the cricketer, with a more rounded and dispassionate study of Gimblett the man, with all his traits and torments. He trusted me enough to want me to put it on paper – for others to judge.

Intelligent though he was, he ran from overbearing responsibility. Several of the Somerset players including the vociferous Bill Andrews tried to encourage him to put his name forward as the county's first professional captain. The idea was unthinkable to him. He had enough to worry about: keeping a careworn eye on his own form and flights of temperament.

On a cold Saturday in May 1976 I was professionally covering a Benson and Hedges match between Gloucestershire and Leicestershire at Bristol. It was a day, I remember, when Ray Illingworth began by complaining that the boundary was too short. The match was well on its way and no one seemed to know where the adjudicator was. I looked at my card. It was Harold Gimblett.

Early in the afternoon I took a stroll round the ground and spotted him. He was a solitary figure, taking no more than a token interest in the game as far as I could see. I hesitantly walked up to him. He put his hand on my shoulder.

'Thank God someone will talk to me.'

He was imagining, I'm sure, that he was being ostracized. More likely he lacked the confidence that chilly May day to share a gregarious drink and a chat with Benson and Hedges representatives and club officials.

In a lugubrious monologue, quietly confidential, Harold told me how he so nearly turned the car back many times as he approached Bristol that morning and how he remained anonymously in the driving seat outside the ground for a long time before he could bring himself to drive in. He wished Benson and

Hedges had never asked him. It was a terrible responsibility choosing the gold award and he knew he would upset a lot of people.

We remained for a long time together and he talked away. Meanwhile Zaheer and David Shepherd were sharing an excellent partnership of 106 and I expected that one of them would get the award. But Leicestershire were bowled out for 156 and skipper Tony Brown (4–31) was Gimblett's choice There were no complaints as far as I knew.

Once before, Gimblett had been adjudicator in Bristol. That was Cup Final day in 1975 when Hampshire won by 67 runs. He remained convinced that he gave the gold award to the wrong man. Gloucestershire, batting second, were all out for 62 in less than 27 overs. Herman took 5–24 so he must have been a reasonable recipient.

Some of the Hampshire party were discreetly surprised. One told me later: 'I should think the adjudicator spent the afternoon watching the cup final.' He didn't.

But Andy Roberts should probably have been the man. He rescued his side when he went in last and figured in a 61-run last wicket stand with Rice: and he followed this up with 3–10 in 8.5 overs. Gimblett drove home that day, regretting his decision.

In pursuit of some explanations for all the imponderables in his acclaimed and anguished life, I have talked to many of his contemporaries: players, friends and relatives. Their affection is unanimous; so, in many cases, are their reservations.

Rita never wholly understood him. They were, however, close and loving. Only once did he forget her birthday. 'When he saw the other cards arriving, he was horrified. And he brought me a special present to make up for it.'

Perhaps we shall never fully understand him and his fellow-sufferers: not even the psychiatrists who tried so hard to assure him that Somerset and cricket still needed him.

Over the years I watched him hooking fast bowlers as if he were tossing hay back at Bicknoller. I watched him buckle the sight-screens before the new-ball bowler had even taken off his sweater.

I watched him jauntily enjoying himself, in a hurry as ever, as third-formers on the cover fence jostled to field the fourth boundary in the over. On the day he scored 310 against Sussex I went out on my parents' front lawn, tried to imitate the lofted straight drive and smashed the lounge window.

The tragedy is that he was able to share too little of the joy and sheer pleasure he brought to the game of cricket.

THE ENIGMA

'That bloody Gimblett . . .'

John Daniell was in turn Somerset's captain, secretary and president. For many years he was the autocratic influence behind the county's cricket. His administrative skills were considerable. He had sporting friends in high places and if, in recruiting newcomers to the team he was subject to mischievous aberrations over geographical qualifications – no side had more aliens, with mythical passports, that swore allegiance to agricultural bastions like Hardington Mandeville and Compton Dundon – his well intentioned guile was never questioned.

Intimidated professionals listened to his roar, kept their distance and confidentially referred to him as 'the Lion of Judah'. Pre-war Somerset, often an outlandish assortment of public school chums, port-flushed military men and old boys home from the Colonial Service needed someone around to make sure they arrived on time and manifested a token integration with the pros.

In this role John Daniell had many virtues. He was an England cricket selector for three years, though many would claim he was a better judge of a rugby player. His opinions as an international rugby selector were always respected; his son, Nigel, still believes there has never been a better judge of a player. Maybe his cricketing instincts were more suspect. He told Gimblett, in his opening weeks at Taunton, that he was not good enough and

11

would not be retained. That rankled for a long time, even when the Daniell assessment mellowed and he offered kindly asides as the young batsman walked past the secretary's window. Some of the Daniell entourage recall discussions that persisted, about the richly gifted but patently unsettled Gimblett, right up to the early Fifties. They could never decide what to make of him as he shrugged off a compliment or told them succinctly his views on committee members.

Surrounded by his cronies, John Daniell would frequently over the years shake his head and say: 'That bloody Gimblett . . .' Such a laconic trinity of evocative words apparently summed it all up, encapsulating the so-called belly-acher, the barrack room lawyer and the prickly private schoolboy who refused to kowtow.

Whatever the quirks, social or political, Harold's inherent element of rebellion was at times much admired by many of the other players. The Twenties and Thirties turned many bright, independently minded young pros into sycophants. That nominal acquiescence helped, if you wanted to keep your place in the team.

Gimblett feared no one in life; the only fright came from the demons that grew in his head. To the onlooker, he was for the most part personable and poised. Spectators always associate carefree aggression at the crease with a sunny disposition.

He could be all these things. John Daniell, who came to extol the prodigious hitting, saw him one way. Fellow professional Horace Hazell saw him as a flamboyant schoolboy and, then in a considered postscript, as the definitive Jekyll and Hyde. Jack Hurley, who went to school with him as a small boy at Williton and later became the esteemed editor of the local weekly paper, said: 'Harold was an infuriating enigma.' It was an observation with affection in the voice.

I, too, saw the many faces of Harold Gimblett. That was part of the fascination of the man. His paradoxes were numberless.

He was the village boy and the sophisticate. Exmoor and the Quantocks tugged at him emotionally. His thick forearms be-longed to Bicknoller at harvest time, even though there is not too much direct evidence of his passion for hard farmwork. In the Somerset dressing room, engulfed by the chirpy, rustic voices of other pros, his accent belonged to West Somerset. But the Gimblett family, especially on his mother's side, had some claims to rural grandeur. Harold and his brothers had been sent to West Buckland School in North Devon: to round off both the character and the voice. He was probably better educated than most of the other professionals. He occasionally read historical biographies and, in the company of the influential and monied around the cricket grounds, he instinctively polished up the vowels. Other players noticed it.

The family had been steeped in agricultural Conservatism. Rita felt Harold was much more of a Liberal; but some of his more outspoken opinions, with no great respect for the status quo had an unmistakable radical ring. In his cassettes he made it clear, however, that he had negligible regard for the leaders of either the Left or the Right.

Unloving he may have been about those who ran the country with what he discerned as a glib and impersonal expediency. Yet cussedly he was also a great Royalist. His wife remembers so well how he hit a six almost the moment Queen Elizabeth II was crowned. It was, she says, a predetermined gesture of patriotism. The showman in him did occasionally threaten to surface like that. On a good day – and there were many of these – he was apt to tell crouching wicket keepers what would happen with the next delivery: and more than that, whether the six would tower towards mid wicket or long leg.

He often appeared to know when he was going to score a century. For a time he was dubbed 'the Saturday cricketer' by his teammates because of a penchant for hundreds just before the weekend. At home, after a melancholy month, he would turn to Rita and say: 'I'm going to get three figures tomorrow.' Usually he did.

The contradictions multiply as we continue to evaluate this extraordinary cricketer. He was one of the most sentimental members of the Somerset team. Soon after the war he was playing

13

at Taunton and in the crowd were some wounded ex-Servicemen. 'I'd done well that day and then went out with Frank Lee to talk to them. One was terribly shot up. He got up with great difficulty, shook me by the hand and thanked me for the enjoyment I'd given him. Then as a spontaneous gesture he suddenly gave me a packet of Woodbines. I had to walk away – I was so overcome with emotion.'

Harold told me of that incident years later. Horace Hazell was also with him at a cricket meeting in Bath during the 1975 Somerset Centenary Year. Gimblett had launched his own appeal to raise money for the county and he was telling his audience how the contributions were arriving, often from people of limited resources. 'A lovely old lady in South Devon sent me the whole of her pension and . . .' Somerset's greatest home-grown cricketer was again in tears.

Once he possessed the country boy's indifference to suffering of animal and bird life. He popped off sparrows and even tom-tits with his air gun; later he made a profitable, if brief, business of rabbit-catching. Like most farmers' sons from Quantocks' territory, he occasionally hunted the graceful stag. In retrospect, such chases filled him with remorse.

I turn again to Mrs Gimblett for this particularly poignant story. 'He told me of the day when a young hind was trapped in a small triangular field. Harold desperately wanted to save it from the hounds. He grabbed it by the neck and tried to calm it. Then the huntsmen arrived, took the hind from him and shot it. He never forgave them. He wanted the deer to live and in the end he had handed it over. He had let the deer down. But at the same time he considered he had been deceived. It showed him how unreliable people could be.'

There are many examples of his kindness, a characteristic sustained through to his last painful days at Verwood in Dorset. He loved small children and the elderly. He could address a village cricket club with gentle, engaging charm, without a hint of swagger or boastfulness. He could be patient with autograph hunters. There were days when, whatever his protestations in

14

later life, he enjoyed the adulation of being Somerset's favourite son.

Yet the lack of grace could also be stunning. Once at Gravesend he made a marvellous 184 against Kent. It won the match for Somerset. Eric Hill was the 12th man and a Kent member said to him: 'I'd very much like to buy that Gimblett a drink.' After a decent pause, the message was relayed to Harold who had been busy criticizing the other members of the team for their inept batting. 'A drink? I don't want one,' he growled. Hill pressed him and eventually he agreed with reluctance to have a lemonade. The member's response to that: 'Heavens, fancy being able to bat like that on lemonade. Best bit of slogging I've ever seen.' Hill adds wryly: 'I didn't report that to his nibs!'

Ben Brocklehurst, Gimblett's last Somerset captain, described him as 'immensely entertaining, warm hearted and a good companion when he was relaxed.' But Brocklehurst, too, was involved in matches which illustrate uncompromising lapses of grace. At Old Trafford when Gimblett had only made a few runs, he heard some prominent members of the Lancashire Club making a disparaging comment on an umpiring decision which favoured Somerset.

Gimblett leaned over the balcony and said: 'Why don't you go back to the bloody mills and do an honest day's work.'

The language slipped that day. So it did at Lord's after an untimely dismissal. As the Somerset batsman walked dejectedly back through the Long Room, an ageing member mumbled: 'I'm sorry you are out, Gimblett. I've come a long way to watch you bat.'

The tactlessness of the remark heightened the class complexes that were never far away when Gimblett played at Lord's. He stopped and glared at the member. 'You ought to have bloody well stayed at home.'

Many professionals would admire his reaction. Cricket has always had too many people making inane comments at the wrong time.

Gimblett was self-critical to a degree. When he was out, the

15

eloquence of his silent displeasure told it all. Mostly he disguised his emotions until he got back to the dressing room. 'We tried to get out before he returned,' one teammate told me. 'He was apt to throw his bat around, not only on the occasions when he had failed.'

From a safe, detached distance, this could be almost funny. The former Somerset amateur Hugh Watts, who first played immediately before the last war and made intermittent appearances until 1952, still chuckles at the mental picture of one or two of the older and wiser professionals 'leading the evacuation from the changing-room when Harold was out'. It seemed to make no great difference, whether he had scored 100 or been out for a duck.

'I'd offer a "Well batted, Harold" or "Hard luck". Either would set off an outburst of general condemnation of either a partner or an opponent, innocent or guilty. He was a bit like a temperamental prima donna. His fellow professionals would leave well alone until the storm had subsided. Then would come the natural humour of Horace, the quiet understanding of Wally and Arthur, the sympathy of Bill, who had similar chips on his shoulder but was always full of admiration.'

Watts, a kindly schoolmaster who bridged the decreasing gap between amateur and professional, was apt to be called Master Hugh before the war. In the process of social evolution around St James Street, the prefix mellowed to Mister and then, in no time at all, a democratic Hugh or an affectionate 'The Abbot'. When he saw Gimblett in the role of spoilt child, Watts reprimanded himself for succumbing to a master's opinion. 'Harold was no longer a schoolboy and who was I to understand and interpret the ways and antics of a near-genius in his early thirties?'

Gimblett would rumble belligerently about an unfriendly act from the opposition or a suggestion of cheating. Eric Hill, a Taunton boy whose cricketing fantasies were realized when he found himself opening with Gimblett for Somerset after the war, recalls: 'Once at Neath some felt I was cheated on a run-out

16

and Harold was absolutely furious – not only about the cheating but also, I think, because in some outlandish way it reflected on his running.'

He liked to see a batsman walk if he knew he was out. So there is a certain irony in one of his club matches for Taunton against local rivals, Bridgwater. Harold was going well with Vic Robson, son of the marvellous Ernie Robson, that taciturn Yorkshireman who played as a pro for Somerset till he was past fifty. Vic hit the ball back; it bounced off the slow bowler and Harold was well run out. He knew it, everyone knew it. The umpire, attached to the Taunton club, shook his head and the batsman sheepishly stayed. Almost the next over, Robson was out to a dubious lbw. at the other end. 'You had to suffer because of me,' said Gimblett with some guilt.

In spite of his enormous natural talents as a batsman, his physical strength, his eagle eye, his innate sense of timing, he could be a soft touch for the opposition. If he was in a bad mood, the runs were less likely to come. There were days when he threw his head in the air to play a thoroughly reckless shot that conveyed both apathy and irresponsibility. He also had the facility, in defiance of a reputation for beefy blows, for intense concentration. After polishing up his defence, so vulnerable in the early seasons, he could unconcernedly put a straight bat to the best of our domestic new-ball bowlers. It should quickly be said that in his contrary flights, he showed a disinclination to demonstrate such application when maybe it was sorely needed. Friends believed he played badly to jeopardize his chances of going on tour.

That theory is hard to substantiate. It is true that he had no great wish to be selected. The reason, I suspect, had more to do with a lack of self-confidence and an ever-present fear of failure than the notorious streak of cussedness. After the war, Wally Hammond inevitably held a good deal of sway. Gimblett's regard for Hammond as a person was somewhat grudging; it was almost certainly mutual.

At the same time, Gimblett felt he had something to prove when Somerset played at Gloucester in the August of 1946. His

17

innings of 133 was crisp, positive and intrepid, a collector's piece and a treat for those who watched at the Waggon Works ground. At the wicket he was loquacious and even impish. He started by turning to Hammond in the slips, after one of his early boundaries, to ask: 'What have I got to do to get on this boat trip of yours then, Wally?' As the score mounted, in an innings more or less flawlessly compiled, he pursued his little joke. 'That should be another step up the gangplank . . .'

Later, he told a friend: 'I reached my century and Hammond said "Sorry, Harold, you've no chance! That innings made no impression." '

We shall never know whether, privately, he wanted it to. But that particular 133, watched at close quarters by England's captain, was a psychological triumph for the Somerset man.

He could be, as I have said, careless and irresponsible. Is it wholly a fair criticism in the case of an opening batsman whose sturdy country shoulders carried, with meagre support, so much of Somerset's fragile batting? So often, single-handed, he took the shine off the ball; so often he retrieved a lost cause. He was, when he wished to be, a superb team man.

I return to Horace Hazell, that endearing roly-poly little left-arm spinner who waited patiently for 'Farmer' White to give up. 'I've no doubt at all about Harold's finest innings. It was against Kent on a dusty Gravesend wicket. He knew that Doug Wright was capable of running straight through us. As he padded up he said that if Doug was allowed to pitch the first ball we'd all be out for 20. Harold walked out to the wicket and decided it was up to him. I think the very first ball he received from Doug was hit full-toss to square leg for six. And the second, turned into a half-volley, was straight-driven for four. He went on to score a wonderful century.'

Wright, hustling along his leg breaks and googlies at almost medium pace, had numerous contests with Gimblett. There was great artistry on both sides. The googlie was known to slip through occasionally. At Gravesend, where the dust was flying, Gimblett was the master. Here was authority, unselfishness and what was perhaps a rare relish for responsibility of this magnitude. Here was batting not far short of genius.

At all times he was a perceptive cricketer. His knowledge of the game, technical and intuitive, was immense. The Gimblett swish at the away swinger or the cocky hook to a surreptitiously placed long leg were imprudent. But he walked to the wicket with a comprehensive grasp, matched by not so many of his contemporaries, of opponents' whims and wiles. He knew all there was to know of the vagaries of specific squares and the likelihood of humidity to help the swingers.

He was the least inhibited of batsmen. Bowlers' reputations never bothered him. 'I was not once in my life afraid of a bouncer,' he said when he started talking into his cassette microphone. His problems, as we cannot repeat too often, were of another kind altogether.

Wherever does one finish in discussing his paradoxes? The introvert who refused to stop talking once he got to the crease (another manifestation of his troubled nervous energy) . . . the puritan who enjoyed the occasional gin-and-tonic and the harmless attentions of an attractive woman . . .

His behaviour in company was always very proper. He rarely swore – and then his hackles were only raised by fatuous and ill-considered words from those who should have known better than prod at his delicate veneer of sensitivity – and he discreetly withdrew from the conversation of the dressing room at the peaks of collective ribaldry. No one would ever have called him narrow-minded, though. Johnny Lawrence, high as the stumps and full of chirpy North Country nonsense, was arguably more so: he advocated abstinence with Nonconformist zeal, softened by a good-natured smile.

Harold Gimblett, within the context of Somerset cricket, was something of a glamorous figure. His maiden century, scored as a greenhorn, was a magnificent story to retell over cocktails. For years he dominated the local headlines and was the most revered cricketer in the county since Sammy Woods. Jack White, in his reliable, phlegmatic way, was a wonderful all-rounder who skippered England. He, too, was a farmboy and his ultimate cricketing journey was even more spectacular than Gimblett's. But his appeal was never magnetic in the same way. Schoolboys did not throw down their satchels to watch him wheel away throughout the afternoon on the county ground.

Gimblett was intermittently a national talking point and always a regional celebrity. At social gatherings, where committee members and their wives gathered after the close of play, he was the centre of attention. He was not a ladies' man but did not discourage the odd suggestion that he might be. 'It didn't cut much ice with us,' one of his fellow professionals told me. Rita said: 'He was a very good-looking young man and I'm sure he had women admirers. That was as far as it got.'

His cricket, many claimed, lacked the killer instinct. It was the difference, they said, between the Saturday afternoon player at Watchet and the Test opener at Lord's. There was, however, a seldom seen compulsion to succeed at all costs, a less prepossessing feature of his multi-faceted personality.

Eric Hill's parents knew how much their son idolized Gimblett. As a special treat for 15-year-old Eric, Harold was invited for tea in 1938. 'He came and we eventually played ping-pong in the small dining room. Harold served with a vicious spin imparted by sliding the ball along the bat in an illegal way and was totally unplayable. He was delighted to beat me out of sight.'

All those aches and pains

Harold Gimblett was the undisputed captain of cricket's hypochondriacs. His shoulders were broad and his complexion healthily bronzed for most of his playing career; but he worried ceaselessly about injury and illness.

Friends used to say, only half in jest, that he was always in the doctor's waiting room in Taunton's Station Road and that his car, suitcases and cricket bag were apt to resemble a chemist's shop. Rita had been trained in pharmacy and the pair believed in taking care. From the days when his mental battles first began noticeably to surface, Harold was prescribed pills. They came in all sizes and colours. He would emphasize his faith in them as he took his allocation between innings. 'The docs know what is best for me,' he would say, with a wry look round the dressing room. In the end, of course, with a cruel and ironic twist, he chose that they should kill him.

Aches and pains, physical and mental, were never far away. There was often a dramatic element to the way he swallowed his tablets and pills. For a man who questioned so much in life, he accepted the rituals of medication with a tacit resignation. He was not sure that the pills were a panacea for all his ills but it reassured him that he usually had a supply in his coat pocket.

In Gimblett's first month with Somerset, R. J. O. Meyer withdrew from the side to play at Lord's because of an attack of malaria – though it could have been a kindly act by that acute psychologist – and the farmer's boy rightly found himself keeping his place after the Lawrence Trophy innings at Frome. Gimblett injured his leg while fielding. It did not stop him scoring a half-century in the second innings, with the help of a runner. Then he was sent off to see a specialist in Harley Street. The leg was massaged and he was given some pain-killer tablets. He sampled them as soon as he was outside.

My goodness, they were strong. They nearly knocked me out. I found myself wandering around the streets of London, not really knowing what I was doing. Eventually I was picked up by a policeman. He thought I was drunk and disorderly. It was all rather embarrassing. But then he recognised me from the recent publicity at Frome and bought me a cup of tea instead!

Such miscalculations of the dosage apart, his hypochondria became a matter of intense and at times jokey interest to his colleagues. He would turn up with a headache and lie down in the dressing room, reluctant to take the field. In fact, he had a history of migraine going back to his days as a small boy in West Somerset.

21

I once asked a well-known post-war Somerset player for his assessment of Gimblett. Succinctly, he replied without any apparent hesitation: 'A wonderful batsman . . . a very intelligent bloke . . . and a first class hypochondriac.'

He was not alone, of course, in the way he dropped his bat theatrically and fixed the bowler with a withering look when a wicked delivery rapped him on the wrist. More significant was the comment of one of the county's amateurs. 'I have known Harold to surrender his wicket after a painful blow.'

His 1950 carbuncle, surely one of the most headlined in the annals of first class cricket, if not medical history, ended collective hopes of a belated Test comeback. We shall refer again later to that unlikely material for journalistic zeal, the boil on the neck. For the time being, perhaps it is reasonable to ask ourselves to what extent the carbuncle was psychosomatic. Did it reflect his disinclination to play for his country again? The West Indies spinners of the day, Caribbean cult figures of the beguiling art, knew he had been recalled to savage them and they were grateful that he stayed away.

For all his whims, his moods and even his moans, Gimblett remained a popular member of the team. The other players admired his bountiful gifts of batsmanship and the cavalier approach which conveyed such a contempt for much of the game's inhibiting theory. They admired and envied the way he took on and tamed the best bowlers, fast or slow. When he struck fiery early deliveries straight back over the head of the disconcerted seamer, they chuckled and led the applause. They shared the crowds' pleasures at the way he excelled in the outfield or, less often, picked up sharp close catches off Wellard, Andrews and Hazell, who were always reassured by the sight of Gimblett at second slip. Certainly there was plenty of evidence that he could be an affable companion in the dressing room or in a hotel restaurant. He had a card-index knowledge of opponents and their tactical and temperamental flaws. When he talked cricket, it was perceptive and demanded attention; but his conversation would frequently veer outside the game.

22

He, in turn, valued the friendship of many of the players. Bill Andrews and Horace Hazell were invited to his wedding. He was always grateful to Arthur Wellard who lent him his spare bat for the dynamic Frome debut. Frank Lee, with whom he opened the innings for so long, was a loyal friend, and so was that efficient and introvert stumper, Wally Luckes. Harold did his best for the various beneficiaries and regretted that he failed twice, within a matter of hours, in Bertie Buse's calamitous benefit match at his native Bath in 1953. By teatime on the first day it was all over and the victorious Lancashire were packing their bags for home. The Somerset ground staff were left sadly surveying the newly-laid pitch; Tattersall was left to cherish his 13–69; and Bertie, most imperturbable of batsmen, was probably a good deal less phlegmatic as he counted the pennies.

Gimblett was later to say to Buse: 'You still did better than I did. Once I'd paid the expenses, I ended up with less than £8 from my benefit match.'

Andrews asked Gimblett to be the godfather to Michael, the son from Bill's first marriage. The duties, in fact, were never quite fulfilled; the journey to the church by the Gimbletts was held up by a tree across the road. The melancholy thread continues: Michael, who was to become a Somerset policeman, took his life in middle age, not so long after Harold's suicide.

Like all groups of people who live in an enclosed community – such as a cricket dressing room – temporary feuds are inevitable. Somerset, stacked with oddball personalities in the pre-war years, had its share. In the years between the wars there were one or two members of the team who had a slightly excessive thirst and at least one other, not Gimblett, whose mental state was not renowned for its equilibrium. As the expansive Andrews was inclined to say amidst barside bonhomie in later life: 'We had the lot – those with the DTs and another one round the bend!'

In his early days with the county, Gimblett would nod in the vague direction of the amateurs' room and say to no one in particular: 'They're a rum lot in there.'

The other players would have liked him to show a more open

interest in their batting. He seldom watched them when he was out. He would retire to the depths of the dressing room or sit in his car. If his tetchy demeanour was evident, they kept their distance. At the same time they warmed enthusiastically to his many moments of personal triumph.

His friendships within the team were constant rather than intimate. Hazell amused him. The left-arm spinner was rotund and singularly unathletic in build. Yet he was the one Gimblett chose as his runner. 'Don't ask me why – it surprised a lot of people. But I was a kind of lucky mascot, I suppose. Harold insisted on me. It was something I could do – and even make a few yards in the process!'

The spectacle of Gimblett smoothing shots through the covers or heaving short-pitched balls down in the direction of long leg, with tubby Hazell loyally scuttling off as the deputy for a well judged two – basking in the effortless grandeur of the stroke as he went – was one to savour.

Gimblett confided to Hazell about domestic matters. 'Things seemed to build up in his mind and grew out of all proportion. It was such a mystery to me. There was really nothing at all to worry about. At other times he was placid and contented, and good, relaxed company.'

The pair had one embarrassing brush. It was after the war at Weston-super-Mare where, not for the only time, the wicket was difficult. Runs were going to be a bonus and Middlesex knew what they had to do. Jack Robertson was going down the pitch and hitting sixes off Hazell: rather a lot of sixes. Horace still relives the agony on that Clarence Park ground, surrounded by conifers and Midland holiday makers up from the beach. 'It was an incredible wicket and what they didn't realize,' Hazell says, 'was that it was just as bad for the bowlers. I couldn't control the ball. I didn't know where it was going once it pitched. The sixes weren't my fault.'

As the players came in, Gimblett suddenly went for Hazell. His tirade of criticism was untypical and unwarranted. 'We both raised our voices and the public row continued as we passed the members in their deck chairs outside the pavilion. It was all very unfortunate. Other players tried to calm things down.'

A few days later Rita Gimblett was chatting to Mrs Hazell. Gingerly, Rita said: 'H (Horace) and Harold have had a row, haven't they?' – 'Em–yes, I think so.' – 'Harold is very upset. He hasn't slept for two nights.'

The wives' conversation was relayed back to Hazell. He wasted no time in approaching Gimblett, to whom he had not spoken since the incident. 'This is so childish, isn't it?' They shook hands on the spot.

More than one observer of the Taunton dressing room scene, especially in the years following the war, felt that there was more than a passing suggestion of jealousy in the Gimblett make-up. Unprompted, they independently cited M. M. Walford as an example. This Triple Blue from Oxford would leave his school-mastering at Sherborne to spend the summer vacation weeks making runs for Somerset. Micky Walford was endowed with great natural gifts as an opening batsman: he wasted no time in accumulating runs with a stylish assurance much to the liking of the local crowds. He walked to the wicket with Harold, middled the ball as if he had been playing county cricket since May and even had the effrontery to outscore his partner at times. The sight of the pair in full flow was an exciting one, indeed. It remains what for me, as a Somerset lad, was one of my most cherished sporting memories. Herbert Hewett, in a hurry, and Lionel Palairet, playing for the poets, must have been a marvellous opening combination for the county: the sepia still of their historic stand of 346 against Yorkshire in 1892 is almost at the top, at least figuratively, in my treasure chest of cricketing heroics. I can shut my eyes and yet see the detail: the two men leaning on their trusted bats in front of the small, improvised scoreboard, Hewett with black shoes beneath his pads as if rushed back to record the feat by an opportunist photographer. They had destroyed Yorkshire that August day, to notify the first class game's remote headquarters that Somerset were to be taken seriously. Hewett and Palairet . . . how I wish I had seen them. But Gimblett and

Walford, the old sweat and the schoolmaster, could be just as majestic and awe-inspiring. In those fleeting, rewarding summers' days when the two were together, county cricket had no better opening pair. Statistics in their inanimate way make the point but tell half the story.

How did Gimblett, the established idol of Somerset, react to this accomplished newcomer with his handsome range of shots and public school manner? I went to Walford himself for the answer. 'The other pros always said that Harold tended to try that bit harder when I was playing. Although we got on very well, when he was out he would storm into the professionals' dressing room and say "Micky is taking all my bloody luck!"'

One of the professionals of that period underlined the point. 'This touch of jealousy did show in August when Micky Walford arrived from Sherborne. According to Harold, Micky was the luckiest batsman of all time. But that was patently untrue.'

Jealousy is not unknown in country cricket; nor is it unreasonable in a game of internal competition, with its accompanying sense of insecurity.

It should be remembered that Gimblett was indisputably Somerset's individual star before and after the war. Spectators came specifically to watch him score runs in his own dazzling fashion. Wellard was loved for his sixes; Buse for his bum-intruding stance and unshakable temperament as solid as the Abbey near the solicitor's office where he used to work; Lawrence for his endearing antics at short leg, and Stephenson for his suicidal singles. But Gimblett was the Master. He had the shots, the timing, the arrogance, the sheer class. Though he was not a braggart, headlines were his preserve. And intermittently others emerged to threaten the Master's elevated station.

Maurice Tremlett must have been one of these. He worked in the office at Taunton before the war and dreamt of being a county cricketer himself. No doubt he ignored the mundane secretarial chores to peer through the window of that once quaint little office and catch the expressions of joy on the members' faces. That told him that Gimblett was going well.

26

Then after the war it was Tremlett's own turn. He was fair haired, broad shouldered and good looking. He could strike an early ball back over the bowler's head. His straight driving could be as exhilarating as Gimblett's; and, significantly, the crowd took to him immediately. In his first appearance at Lord's, as a professional cricketer, he won the match on his own. The members rose to him. Soon – and this is not the place to ponder the folly of such premature judgements – he was being likened to great England all-rounders. His Test recognition deservedly followed, though his international career was curtailed by conflicting counsel from those in high places, who watched him in the West Indies and gave this fine, natural bowler, added complexes rather than technique.

Gimblett was a wary observer of the Tremlett progress. It did not help when mutual friends said: 'Young Maurice has got the right idea, Harold. He can hit just like you.'

The two were never especially close. After play on away matches, Gimblett was one of the quiet group. He would perhaps opt for a cinema visit or a stroll round the town. Tremlett preferred a more affable evening. That should not denote antagonism. Cricketers fall into social groups that conveniently reflect their temperaments. There are seldom real political factions.

Eccentric Somerset

The Gimblett tongue could be cutting and dismissive when it came to an opinion of a lesser mortal. But that was his style. He was not a hypocrite: the disparagement would as likely be directed at an unfriendly club official as a struggling pro. A young member of the club, confronted with technical problems over his batting and despairing of success, was just occasionally taken on one side. More often, the Gimblett advice had a grimly realistic edge to it. 'One day,' Ben Brocklehurst told me, 'I heard Harold telling some of the young and newly joined professionals that they would do better to go off and get themselves another job.'

It was not meant, I am sure, in an unkind way. His regard for cricket was never a romantic one. He believed there were better jobs around. The role of the professional cricketer, he argued, carried no status. More than once in his melancholy memories, he said: 'We were the lowest of the low.'

He was apt to cite the traditional imbalance between the amateurs and the professionals at Somerset, though I am sure other counties have equally bizarre tales to tell of erstwhile public school second XI players hiding their embarrassment under their kaleidoscopic caps as affluent paters nodded in ignorance and perfunctory approval through the tavern window.

Gimblett's assessment of the county's long line of amateur skippers varied enormously; but then so did that of most of the other pros, just as long as they were not overheard. In the early years of the century, Woods, Palairet and Daniell rapidly followed each other as captain. It is true that White, Reggie Ingle and 'Bunty' Longrigg gave some stability to the leadership after that. Yet in 1948 the county were again running through their captains faster than spinners Tom Goddard and Sam Cook were building triumphant sand castles at Bristol. No one seemed to want the job for keeps in that extraordinary 1948 summer; in the end, N. S. Mitchell-Innes, G. E. S. Woodhouse and J. W. Seamer did it between them. Well, more or less. As it happened, Fred Castle, a Man of Kent like Wellard, and Hugh Watts also took charge for the occasional match. It was civilized country-house cricket, disconcerting only for the players who wondered aloud about the batting order and the permutation of the bowlers.

Later, if not quite with as much indecent haste, came Stuart Rogers, Brocklehurst and G. G. Tordoff, by which time Gimblett had gone. Some of the appointments were surprises; some of the nominees were not very good at all, either as captains or players.

R. J. O. Meyer, then headmaster of Millfield, where he administered with much skill and was known to impart racing tips to favoured boys, skippered Somerset for a single season, 1947. The players were genuinely sorry that back trouble ruled him out after that. Here was a captain worth his place. He used to open the bowling for Cambridge and first played for Somerset in 1936. If he had not wandered off to India he might have played for England. Flummoxed batsmen, not to say wicket keepers, said he was quite capable of bowling six varieties an over. His theories were just as engaging and eccentric. On a rainy afternoon he would persuade the players to vacate their card schools and move their chairs around the pavilion as Jack Meyer paraded his latest theories about field-placings.

One favourite story, related by Horace Hazell, is of the intense preparation, inspired by Meyer, that went into a match against Middlesex at Lord's. Somerset had seven bowlers in those days and the skipper had worked out the ideal placings for all of them. 'You won't need to ask me – you'll know where to go,' he told them. And, indeed, as the West Countrymen, never renowned for their agility, took up their positions with such precision for one bowler after another, the M.C.C. members began looking at each other with undisguised admiration. Then suddenly came chaos. In came J. T. Eaglestone and he was a left-hander. And that was something 'R.J.O.' had forgotten all about.

That story may have been marginally embroidered with the needles of affection. Gimblett, Wellard, Andrews, Hazell and the rest said there was nothing apocryphal about the occasion skipper Meyer blithely pulled the communication cord on the Manchester express after a tiring day in the field. The perplexed guard hurried along to the compartment. 'We're members of Somerset County Cricket Club, old chap. One or two have said they're starving. D'you think you could rustle anything up?'

Everyone said R.J.O. was a splendid manager. Miraculously some food turned up, the train puffed off on its way again and there is no record of a fine imposed on either Somerset or its captain for stopping the express.

Gimblett shared the chuckles of his teammates at many a cricket gathering when Meyer's name was mentioned. In more than a hundred years, Somerset have had good captains in between the undistinguished ones. For sheer imagination, Meyer was high

29

on the list. He could predict vagaries of the wicket as well as a winner at Wincanton.

A number of the county's captains told me at varying times that Harold was not easy to handle. It was a statement of fact, not especially a criticism. Without exception they emphasized his immense value to the team and the stresses through which he lived – and batted.

Brocklehurst, the last captain under whom Gimblett played, says: 'I shall always remember him with affection as well as respect. The team realized his problems and were genuinely fond of him. It was a tragedy that a brilliant cricket career should be marred by a mental illness over which the poor fellow had no control.'

In truth, Harold was slightly wary of Ben Brocklehurst. One player told me: 'Ben was quite strong and you couldn't play around with him. He got on to Harold once or twice.' We shall discuss later those sad final days when, with Brocklehurst in charge, Gimblett eventually packed his bags and left.

Relationships within the larger Gimblett family – and its offshoots – could be both strong and tenuous. Harold's warmth towards his wife and only son, Lawrence, was evident enough. Yet in the closing months of his life he seemed to worry about this and analysed such intimacies.

Lawrence was born in 1943. I was on duty at the fire station at the time. The matron rang me and said 'You have a son.' It just didn't register at first – I was so tired. I think I really wanted a daughter . . . I would probably have liked Lawrence to be a good cricketer although I never attempted to influence him. When I asked him whether he wanted to be a cricketer, he said he thought it was a stupid game. I accepted it. But it possibly brought a slight barrier between us. I have two lovely grandchildren and couldn't see them often enough . . .

My wife has had a lot to put up with but we're still together. I said so many biting, even vicious, things to her. We're closer now than at any time in our life.

30

His dealings with the newspapers could be cordial or bristly. He harboured a grievance about the way EC4 heightened and elongated the drama of his maiden century. At the time he cringed from the ballyhoo. He knew it would be impossible to live up to. Friends teased him about journalists and photographers chartering planes to see him on the farm. He never forgave the press. That accounted for some of his more caustic stage whispers when well-intentioned reporters were around.

He was always sensitive to criticism and any cricket writer who dared to suggest that a particular shot had been rash or untimely would be forewarned that 'Gimbo' was on the warpath. 'The trouble with you people is that you expect me to hit a century every time I go out to the wicket. And when I fail, you can't wait to give me some stick.'

That was just not true. He was idolized in the West Country press, and evening papers were inclined to keep his name in type for the next headline. Many national writers, too, had a consistent regard for him and advocated his recall when the selectors seemed to suffer from the delusion that there was no county west of Middlesex. He remained, whatever his own attitudes to the game, a romantic figure, a dashing hero and a mighty hitter. He epitomized the stirring notion that every match was won with a six. And newspapers mostly loved him for it. Regional journalists gave him the number of column inches that Ian Botham was later to command.

His jaundiced views about the press could be very naive.

I hate the way the press sit in judgement. Most of them haven't played the game. They pillory players. The things they say about players, the viciousness of it . . . I have played cricket for fifty years and never known anyone deliberately drop a catch. Why must the press name them when a catch goes down? I will say to you the only bit of Latin I know: Humanum est errare . . . It is human to err.

Those thoughts, surely, come from Gimblett's own experiences. There were catches he dropped and he was named. The argument is a frail one. Most of my press box colleagues, too, have been active cricketers at some level. I never cease to be gratified by their devotion to the game. Cricket writers are an impassioned breed. They bring their record books with them; their obsession for cricket is both academic and emotional. I wish Harold had eavesdropped more often.

Part of their job, however, is to be detached and unsentimental. Just as a brilliant catch is mentioned, so should be a dropped one. A paid sportsman cannot expect to be shielded, just because he did not try to put the ball on the ground. Robertson-Glasgow, claimed Harold, never named the hapless fielder. Compassionate as he was by nature, I cannot quite believe that of Crusoe.

If Robertson-Glasgow was 'the peer' of cricket writers, who came after him in Gimblett's opinion? 'Neville Cardus was second . . . Ron Roberts third . . . and Jim Swanton fourth.'

The late and highly regarded Ron Roberts loved Somerset and got to know Gimblett well. 'After Ron had done his National Service he came up to me and said he wanted to be a cricket writer. Could I help him? I told him to read all the reports of Robertson-Glasgow he could get his hands on.'

Crusoe wrote hundreds of words about Gimblett. Perhaps he distilled as well as anyone the real man and cricketer. He was, said Robertson-Glasgow, a person possessed of the yeoman's independence. 'As a batsman, he has never let art get above itself.' In that same essay, he wrote:

This is not an indictment of selectors, an old if innocent pastime. It is an attack, rather, on the modern outlook, on the mistaken theory that there can be no place in a major Test match for the batsman who is colloquially in a hurry. This theory is wrong in three important ways. It discourages the making of those strokes from which are born the joy of batsmanship, and imposes on Test cricket a technique of mere safety which would not be endured in an ordinary county game. It encourages the enemy's bowlers by relieving them of the opposition of shock, and by allowing them too high a conceit of their own abilities. Worst of all, it surrenders to the pernicious idea of a record-hunting age that runs are in themselves more valuable than the manner, the period and the occasion of their making.

Crusoe, a useful inswing bowler who rather fancied himself opening the innings – a rare treat he even enjoyed once or twice for Somerset, probably as the result of some persuasive talking the night before – was one of cricket's lovely humorists. He had the sensitivity of the poet (which he was) and preferred writing about the players' whims, quirks and warm hearts than the number of runs they scored. He made other players laugh when he fielded alongside them; when he came back to Taunton or Bath as a journalist, he often hunted Harold out and made him laugh. Not everyone could do that.

Some said Gimblett had no great sense of humour. Somerset colleagues are divided on that. But then cricket is not often a laughing matter throughout the season. Ducks, bad lbw. decisions, snicked fours, dropped catches, nervous overthrows and outfielding in the sweltering heat are not funny. My own observations led me to believe that Gimblett had a dry sense of humour and it was inclined to carry a sting in the tail. The jokes came from a naturally weary voice but it would be quite wrong to say that he was humourless. I know that Rita Gimblett, who as her husband said 'put up with so much,' would agree with me.

Frank Lee was one of the quiet gentlemen of Somerset cricket. His speech was gentle and dignified. So was his batting. He plodded efficiently on with an air almost of reproach as Gimblett flashed his brazen bat. Let no one undervalue his worth to the county: he scored 23 centuries, mostly at his own pace. He was an unselfish cricketer and was happy to leave the six-hitting histrionics to Harold. They were friends on and off the field and used to share little jokes about their varying styles.

The sight of them opening the innings was reassuring. Spectators knew that if Gimblett was in the mood to disturb the fish in the Tone and perhaps not be around for too long, the sedate left-hander Lee would redress the balance.

'Do you know, on several occasions I reached 50 before Harold,' he chuckles in mock reprimand. 'In 1946 at Trent Bridge, Somerset followed on 200 behind and it was not long before I was past 30 and he was 3. Harold wanted to know what was going on. I replied that they were bowling me half-volleys all the time. So it went on . . . 50 to 25, 80 odd to 50, 98 to 74 . . . It really looked as though I was going to be first to the century. But for a time after that I received no bowling and Harold got to 98. Freddy Stocks came on and bowled a long hop. And Harold was caught at third man!'

Lee tactfully draws a veil over the Gimblett reaction. They joked about it many times in the years to come. With typical modesty, the left-hander failed to add that he went on to score 169, his highest innings.

There were always riotous elements to the way the professionals used to share rooms in recommended digs on away matches – to save on their expenses. Mother Nye's was a favourite establishment for impecunious cricketers who in some cases considered adequate beer money almost as important as the comfort of a bed for the night. Many of the Somerset players stayed there at some time: 3/6 a night, and three rashers and two eggs in the morning.

It could mean sleeping two or even three in a bed. Bill Andrews has written hilariously of the time Somerset were playing at the Oval and four of the team crammed into a single room at Paddington. Bill and Horace Hazell, who both tell the story with relish, still vividly remember how three of them squeezed into one double bed. The portly Horace had a small bed all to himself in that postage-stamp room.

The night was humid and sleep fitful. Andrews and Wellard woke as one to find Gimblett throwing open the window and saying to no one in particular in the darkened Paddington street below: 'I can't sleep . . . I can't sleep. My head's buzzing. I'm still making too many runs!'

He was, in fact, going through a prolific period and had been

34

neurotically reliving many of his shots from the previous innings. The other three occupants, generous to a fault, decided in a touching show of democracy that Harold was the man in form and should have the small bed from then on. For the rest of that sweaty and fretful night, Messrs Wellard, Hazell and Andrews made up professional cricket's most comically horizontal threesome.

Cricket for the pros was a pragmatic business. After an evening's steady drinking, the nocturnal emptying of the chamber pot was a necessary ritual. The contents were usually deposited out of the window.

Once, in Harrow Road digs, the good-natured landlady expressed genuine concern about small stone objects in the chamber. She feared for the well-being of the occupants' kidneys. After furtive examination they were able to reassure her with the news that the stones were nothing more than the contents of Hazell's trousers, which had fallen in.

Without the extrovert traits of some of his more boisterous teammates and room-mates, Gimblett enjoyed much of the spontaneous humour that came with improvised living during away matches. He did not join the beery banter when the lights were eventually put out but he chuckled away quietly to himself as he lay in bed. That was really true of the pre-war days before laughter became more and more submerged in his tormented head.

His own wedding, for all its Methodist respectability, had moments of surrealism that would have fitted into a Monty Python script thirty or more years later. The ceremony itself carried all the necessary restrained dignity of the occasion. The hymns were sung with a wholesome joy; the happy couple smiled shyly at each other as they stood side by side in the central aisle; outside the family photographers waited for a picture of the West Country's famous young cricketer and his bride.

Andrews and Hazell, one dwarfing the other, beamed at the rest of the congregation. Wedding receptions were convivial gatherings and the pair were already working up a thirst. Back at the hotel, however, their bronzed, expectant faces clouded. They realized too late that good Nonconformists had long ago signed the pledge. There was a token bottle of port but the overall atmosphere was one of cordial abstinence.

The two Somerset bowlers, such a comic contrast in size, liked a drink as much as a responsive wicket. Their beer-consuming capacity was in the prodigious class, and here they were, at a Methodist wedding reception, self-consciously gripping in their large bowlers' fists a midget measure of alien port for the toast. The situation called for resourcefulness. They stole away to the bar and ordered two bottles of sherry; and, I understand, asked for the cost to be added to the bill for the reception. Clearly the sherry was seen as legitimate expenses. When Harold later heard of the subterfuge, there were no complaints from him.

His teammates, fortified by their surreptitious sorties to other corners of the hotel, integrated among the other guests with jovial courtesy. Then they set off to keep a requested date with W. G. Penny, the Watchet tailor who had in many ways been Gimblett's mentor and had done so much to advocate a place for him in the county side. By this time Mr Penny was in poor health and the high-spirited cricketers were determined to brighten him up and help him to share, from his sick bed, the festivities of the occasion. 'W.G.', for all his good nature, was also a Methodist and no friend of the demon Drink.

Horace discreetly overlooks one or two of his more extravagant gestures of jollification before a startled Mr Penny. But he does recall: 'That wonderful old man didn't drink himself but his housekeeper ingeniously found a hidden supply of homemade wine and offered it to us. It really was dreadful stuff but by now we weren't too discriminate. That after the two bottles of sherry . . .'

There was still a long night ahead. By a devious route they set off for Bill's local at Weston-super-Mare, having broken the hugely good-humoured journey with a stop for more refreshments at a Brent Knoll pub. By now, Horace had his wife-to-be with him once more; she ensured a few hours later that he was bundled into the train at Weston, bound for Temple Meads station, Bristol.

36

Hazell, with the contented smile of a Brislington lad who had just spun Somerset to victory after the Taunton wicket dried out, promptly fell asleep. He woke drowsily as the train rattled to a halt back in Bristol. He opened the door and steam billowed up from nowhere, engulfing him. 'I can't see . . . I can't see,' he wailed with laughable understatement.

At the same time he stepped out – and dropped. His generous girth broke the fearsome fall to the lines far below. Instead he remained suspended in mid air, his stomach wedged between the passenger step and the edge of the platform. His feet dangled helplessly. As a porter eased him to safety, Hazell summoned up a grin and informed no one in particular: 'It was a lovely wedding. Good old Harold!'

Gimblett probably did not approve of everything he heard about his animated colleagues' behaviour. But the vision of Hazell's bizarre discomfiture at Temple Meads always made him laugh out loud.

Cricket bulges, of course, with happy anecdotes. There are stories about Sammy Woods, Sydney Rippon, Len Braund, Jack Meyer and Bill Alley; there are not many funny stories directly about Harold Gimblett. His aggressive batting still had a slightly stern-faced dignity about it. He was a controlled smiter of fours and sixes rather than a reckless swashbuckler. Many players, if asked what they remembered about him apart from the devastating batting, would say: 'The way he never stopped talking.'

From the moment he reached the crease – often on his journey to the wicket – he chatted away. It conflicted with his basically introvert nature. Psychiatrists may have their own explanation. It was reassuring for him to build up an instant rapport with the opposing fielders. Opposing sides, including Gloucestershire on occasions, decided it was silly to give him the psychological fillip he needed. They discouraged conversation with him; that was good, old steely professionalism, not unfriendliness. His chatting was a by-word in our domestic game.

He knew it. Long after he had finished playing he found himself at a cricket evening with that decidedly talkative Aussie,

Bill Alley, who had come all the way to England – like Woods before him – to learn how to play skittles and discover how short the Taunton boundary really was. Harold turned to Bill and said: 'Just as well you and I weren't ever at the crease together. We'd have talked so much that they wouldn't have been able to get on with the match.'

The company chuckled at the thought of it. Harold paused and then added: 'And if Godfrey Evans had been keeping wicket, there would have been no chance of any play at all!'

Evans equalled Gimblett as a crease-side conversationalist. When the two were together, one crouched benevolently behind the stumps, the banter must have been heard at times on the boundary fence.

Perhaps Godfrey was the greatest talker of all. We used to start our repartee at 11.30 and often kept going most of the day. We never stopped – until I was out. He was also the best coach I ever had. I'd say, 'There's something adrift, Godfrey,' and he'd say, 'I'll put you right, Master.' He always called me Master and still does. I felt I had to talk to someone. It's such a lonely place out in the middle.

. . . There were the occasions when I was scoring with the hook off Trueman. Fred came down the wicket. Eyeball to eyeball. 'If you do that again, I'll pin thee to the sightscreen.' I didn't say anything. The game continued and I hit him for two fours through the covers. He was furious. 'Hey, who taught thee to hook like that, by the way?' I told him it was a Yorkshire-man, name of Herbert Sutcliffe. He never went out of his way to bowl me bouncers again. We had a bit of fun together. Occasionally he won the battle, sometimes I got runs against him.

I was apt to say: 'Come on, Fred, give us a bouncer to get the crowd going.' Then I'd go through the motions of agitation and would seem to threaten him. That would start the Taunton crowd. And Fred would say: 'Hark at them silly buggers. They don't even know what it's all about, do they.'

38

Leslie Angell, a quiet, charming Somerset man from Norton St Philip, played most of his cricket for Lansdown, the old-established Bath club side. He was a neat, stylish opener with the right sense of discrimination to cope with the new ball. In club matches he was a prolific scorer and actually played 132 times for the county in the late Forties and early Fifties. He admitted, like Eric Hill and other local lads, that it was an undeniable thrill to walk out with Gimblett.

Angell had some tidy shots but it was his application, rather than flamboyant range of strokes, that made him a useful foil for Gimblett.

'Only once did I get in front of Harold with the scoring,' he remembers. 'It was in a Bank Holiday match and things were going right for me. His reaction was not by what he said but what he didn't say!'

Gimblett was never wholly at ease against good inswing bowling. His bogey bowler was Gloucestershire's George Lambert, a Londoner with a chirpy sense of humour and, for a relatively small man, the ability to bounce the ball. He shared the new ball with his friend Colin Scott and very nearly went on one of the trips to Australia.

In 1950, Gimblett walked out with Angell to open the innings at Bristol. He was talking well and in good humour. 'Do you know, Les, I think this bloke Lambert is going to get me again. Two years ago he bowled me first ball in this fixture and last summer he got me second ball. Let's see what happens with the third ball this morning.'

And what did happen? Lambert moved the ball, Gimblett was deceived and Basil Allen took the catch at short leg.

The batsman shook his head in self-reprimand before exchanging a glance with the bowler. Then, as if remembering what he had said minutes before, he looked at Angell and shrugged. He saw the funny side later.

Rather anti-social he may have been on many a summer's morning, as he took a pill or indicted a committee member. But the unpredictability of his manner was a constant source of fascination and wonderment to the other players. He might be glum one day; yet the next, he was just as likely, in the ways of Wellard, to wander into the other team's dressing room and joke about the state of the game.

In dominating the Somerset batting for so long, he found himself with an unlikely assortment of partners. Once he made almost 100 runs while Hazell was there with him at No. 11. The bowlers had virtually given up trying to remove Gimblett. 'Don't do anything daft, H. Just stay there,' he told Horace. It was a role that the tailender could adopt with great aplomb: in fact, he never discouraged suggestions that he was the best No. 11 in the country. The fielders crowded the bat and suddenly Hazell cut loose with several wicked pulls that had the short legs ducking in antics of self-preservation. That amused Gimblett who promptly trotted down the wicket for a slap on the back and one of his stage-whispered compliments, in this case not exactly to the liking of the bowler or the close fielders.

To see a late-order batsman rising dramatically above the indignity of his station was something to make Harold chortle. So were lucky snicks from his colleagues – the kind that brought groans of exasperation from the suffering seamer. At Birmingham soon after the war, opener Hill was in all sorts of trouble against Tom Pritchard and Charlie Grove on what was a quick and lively wicket. When he edged one high over the slips, he looked suitably contrite and sheepish.

Gimblett immediately came marching down the pitch and said loudly: 'Come on, me son, look as though you meant it.'

Whether or not the remark was meant to have a patronizing edge, only Hill will know. There were not too many tips passed on to younger players by Gimblett, and praise and encouragement seemed a trifle grudging. That, however, was an attitude not confined to cricket. Professional sportsmen are a defensive and insecure breed; they become lop-sided from habitually looking over their shoulders to see who is coming up to take their contract in a couple of years' time.

Gimblett welcomed praise himself, though he accepted it at

times with an undisguised modicum of cynicism in the voice. He took technical advice with reluctance, unless it came in the form of those kind and generous words from Hobbs, Hendren or Sutcliffe. John Daniell told Gimblett to delete the hook shot from his developing repertoire and the counsel was privately resented. It was, in fact, given in good faith. J. C. W. MacBryan, a stylish opener for Somerset – with a superb square and late cut – was in no more favour than Gimblett when it came to Test selectors. He knew them socially and understood the way their minds worked. It did not help him: he played once only for England and then the match, against South Africa at Old Trafford, was virtually rained off. MacBryan was an amateur and played in an earlier decade than Gimblett. They both spoke their mind and had an unwavering antipathy towards those in charge at Somerset. In the end, they both turned their back on the county. 'I saw Gimblett, in his early days with Somerset, playing the hook shot at Lord's. I knew that would never do. I thought it would prejudice his Test chances. So what I thought was for his own good, I wrote to him. I got no reply.'

This book is an attempt to discover why he rejected advice like that – the hook served him with exciting fallibility, and many of his devotees are rather glad it did – and why he was wary of competition within his own team; why there was not more laughter from him, of the kind I have cited, to complement the gentle and sensitive nature; why a broad-shouldered cavalier lifted the spirits of a doting community around the Quantocks, the Poldens and the Mendips, and yet withdrew to private tears.

It is time now to turn to Bicknoller – to the Gimblett roots and boyish ruminations.

The boy follows the man in my story but that is no more illogical than the twists in his own complex life.

THE BOY

First six: match abandoned

Harold sat down to talk into his cassette microphone for the first time at 4.45 in the morning. That, whether by design, subconsciously, or a supernatural freak, was the exact hour of the day when he was born at Blake's Farm, Bicknoller on 19th October 1914. He dispassionately noted the coincidence.

> I was the youngest of three boys. When there are three of one, the youngest is never wanted . . . I was to discover that I was the odd man out. There was something a little wrong. I was to be an introvert, a loner . . .

So the complexes, most of them unsubstantiated, were always there. In truth, the doctor claimed that Harold was the most muscular baby he had ever delivered. Every farmer looks for strong sons to carry on the tradition. Percy Gimblett, the father, gazed approvingly at the baby's sturdy limbs. Louise, his wife, said: 'Isn't he well built!'

The Gimbletts, overlooking a variation or two in the spelling of the name, have been living in the area since the fifteenth century. For several generations they had been farmers. Harold's parents were not without reasonable means and they inclined towards what would be called now an upmarket approach to life. They chose to pay for their sons to complete their education at West Buckland School in North Devon. The oldest of the three brothers, Lewis, was to take over the farm when the father died in 1936; the second brother, Dennis, eventually became a clergyman.

Harold was given an equal amount of love and attention by his parents but could not be shaken from his quirkish belief that he was the outsider. He grew into an introspective boy, who spent hours on his own walking across the fields in self-induced loneliness. 'I learned two things in those days,' he would later say, 'the basic laws of the countryside – and how to throw.' He threw stones, apples and conkers with deadly accuracy; he never lost the art as a cricketer.

When visitors called at the farm he vanished, only to reappear much later when his confidence had been restored. He was from choice a silent boy who seldom entered into the conversation of the day. The brothers, Dennis and Harold in particular, would play cricket in the orchard. They frequently used the trunk of an apple tree as a wicket. The contours of the Quantocks stood between the boys and the distant county ground but the Gimblett brothers pretended they could hear the applause. Their sun-lit fantasies complemented the orchard's rosy apples that hung all around them like suspended cricket balls.

According to Dennis, the pair of them went into the orchard with their little bat and tennis ball 'hour after hour, day after day'. It was a surprisingly serious business. They had marked out a reasonable wicket between the trees. Dennis did most of the bowling and kept a good length. A sixpence was placed on the pitch, where the ball was intended to land. For a ten-year-old boy, Dennis maintained the kind of accuracy that encouraged his brother to play assuredly off the front foot. They openly criticized each other. The batting was instinctive but it had to look right. 'Even then, Harold had this flair for hitting the ball very hard indeed. Time and again he'd send it far over the orchard fence. I used to notice those long arms of his – and an eye he inherited from our father who was such a good shot.'

It was Dennis, a gentle, articulate man, who wrote to me from

Australia (and I could picture a twinkle in those faraway eyes): 'It's the only glory I have got – I taught Harold how to play!'

He had every reason to bask in a little of that glory when, newly ordained, he sat in the Eastbourne crowd to watch Somerset's opener score 310.

Blakes Farm, with its Virginia creeper and its honey-coloured thatch, was a cosy, good-looking building. It was grand enough to have its own modest grass tennis court. That has gone long ago; so have the orchards and the walnut trees. A year or so before he died, in one of his enigmatic spasms of sentimentality, he again drove up the winding little lane with his wife. He stopped the car and gazed up at the small-framed window of his old bedroom. He pointed out where he picked watercress in the stream and Rita reminded him where she was chased by a sow when helping to pick up apples. 'And do you remember when you presented me with a basket of golden plums . . . and picked white violets for me?'

Harold was a romantic after all, though it was a facet of his nebulous personality that fellow players hardly knew existed.

On that return to the farm, his birthplace more than sixty years before, he was sad to see the changes. 'Where have all the trees gone? Where's that lovely old fir at the bottom of the garden? Why have the orchards and hedges been flattened? Why is everything looking so gaunt these days?'

He spent a long time gazing across the mauve-carpeted Quantocks and then back across the climbing Brendons on the other side. His roots tugged emotionally at him. He looked at Rita and silently drove away.

Harold knew the feel and the smell and the sounds of this segment of West Somerset too well.

His first school was at Williton and he walked the three miles there and back. Mr Gard, the benign headmaster, forgave him when he was late. The boy was strong and athletic for his age. He could run home all the way without stopping but he preferred to vary the route: to lean over a gate or stretch for birds' eggs. The gabled Williton school, with its two large rooms split into four classes each, was very much to his liking. There was a leisurely, rural feel to the place, and the silver birches gave it a graceful, dignified identity. He excelled in few subjects and at the end of school hurried away, invariably on his own.

He was sorry when Mr Gard retired. The headmaster had no sooner waved goodbye than he set about fulfilling a long-standing ambition. He was determined to learn how to drive a car. As the first step, eagerly observed by Harold, he went off and bought a second-hand motor from the garage in the main street.

For anyone who doubts whether Harold Gimblett ever had a sense of humour, I recommend his version, recalled from innocent boyhood, of what happened when Mr Gard went for his first driving lesson.

'Arthur, one of the mechanics at the garage was going to give him instructions. For the first lesson he was gingerly eased into the driving seat and shown how to engage gears. The gear stick came off in his hand! Lesson deferred. When it came to the second lesson, the stick had been welded back on and Arthur was taking no chances. The car was now parked for safety's sake in the garage – and I was peeping round the door. All Mr Gard had to do was engage the gears and the car would go straight out of the garage onto the street. It was pointing in the right direction. He listened solemnly to all the instructions and climbed in alongside an anxious Arthur. He started the engine with a tremendous roar as if he was on the grid at Brooklands. But he'd put it into reverse – and with an almighty lurch it thundered backwards onto four oil drums on which a baker's van was delicately propped for running repairs. The van clattered to the ground. Mr Gard's new car stalled. White-faced, he stepped out.'

Young Gimblett suppressed his laughter at a scene out of the Keystone Kops. Mr Gard looked at his tutor. 'What – what have I done, Arthur?'

'You went the wrong way, Mr Gard.'

The retiring headmaster made an instant decision. He would never try to drive again. 'I think he gave the car to Arthur on the spot.'

Mr Gard's successor as Williton head was less understanding

about Gimblett's late arrivals. But at least Mr White allowed the lad from Blakes Farm to post his love letters. In the Seventies, more than half a century later at a barn dance organized in aid of Somerset county cricket, a woman pleasantly introduced herself to Harold and said she was Mr White's daughter.

'Goodness gracious!' said Gimblett. 'Perhaps I'm the reason for you being here . . .'

It was Mr White who gave the boy his first game of organized cricket.

I was eight or nine and Mr White arranged the match on Williton Rec ground. My father had actually ploughed and harrowed and levelled that ground. He'd also hauled the special 'rabbits pee' turf from near Bicknoller for laying the nearby bowling green. For my first cricket match, we had four stumps and one pad for each batsman. We had to play on the edge of the holy acre. I went in first and clipped the third ball into Jones's orchard. That was the first six recorded by Gimblett. But we failed to find the ball and the game was abandoned.

Two years later any vague thoughts of pursuing his aptitude for cricket were almost ended altogether. He was chopping wood at home when he severely cut his kneecap. It was stitched together on the kitchen table.

The relationship with his parents was unexceptional. In retrospect, he had a great admiration for his father. 'He was a truly good man and I can't remember him ever doing anyone any harm. Once he lent a pair of horses and a wagon for two fellows to take home some wood for chopping up, after an old elm had blown down in the gale. They loaded the wagon too high and it was cruel on the horses. One of the horses died as a result and I cried at the time. My father shrugged it off and bore no one a grudge. His philosophy was that lenders were probably always losers.'

Harold was more withdrawn than most boys of his age; he was suspicious of strangers. He liked his own company best, walked aimlessly away from the farmhouse along Gypsy Lane many light evenings, and lay in the fields, his head in his hands, when he had an attack of migraine. 'Harold's got one of his headaches,' his mother used to say sympathetically. He hated anyone to fuss over him.

But he had a country boy's sense of mischief. 'P.C. White once gave me a belt around the ears and I never came back a second time,' he told me. He rather approved of that kind of summary justice.

Bicknoller's pragmatic custodian of law and order made sure there was a minimum of juvenile delinquency. Young Gimblett incurred his wrath for a boyish prank one Guy Fawkes day in the early Twenties.

The barber used to come over from Watchet to cut hair in back rooms. Harold had brought some crackers and he tiptoed round to the rear of a cottage where the barber was lathering his village customer. The boy dropped a firework through the open door and scarpered. John, the barber, chased after him, with shaving brush in one hand and cut-throat razor in the other. The customer, his face half covered in lather, joined in. 'I thought it was funny. P.C. White didn't.'

Farm boys learned how to shoot as surely as they learned how to milk a cow. Harold took out a licence for his double-barrel gun when he was only ten. He timorously went to the post office at Williton; no questions were asked. Already he was a good shot. The larder was never empty. The hills at the back of the farm were running with rabbits. He sold them, two for sixpence, to a local hotel which was conveniently run by a relative of his mother.

He also borrowed a .22 rifle and there are a few stories which fortunately did not find their way back to Farmer Gimblett and his wife. Williton school pal Jack Hurley, who became one of the doyens of West Country provincial journalism, once wrote a somewhat tongue-in-cheek story in his weekly paper, about indisputable shot marks on the weather-cock of the Bicknoller parish church. He mischievously wondered whether someone, after a few glasses of potent local apple juice, had mistaken the weather-cock for a pheasant. Years later, Harold admitted to Jack that he was in fact the reckless youth who peppered the weather-vane.

As he described his fleeting act of high-spirited vandalism: 'I started by peppering the back side of the vane and it spun one way. Then I did the same to the front, before it swung the other way. Finally I got it in the middle!'

The mystery of the parish church weather-cock remained unsolved for many years. A wide range of theories, some vaguely connected with the occult, were put forward. After telling me, almost sheepishly, Harold said: 'I do hope the Bishop doesn't charge me for a new one.'

I went back to take a look. The three distinct holes can still be seen. They remain something of a talking point among visitors. Parishioners claim not to know the origins. The Church, in my experience, does not lack a sense of humour. Perhaps a tablet on the wall of the nave could record the fact: 'The weather-cock outside was playfully damaged by Somerset's greatest cricketer, once an inhabitant of this parish.'

There is already an unostentatious tablet on one of the pews. It says that 'William Temple, Archbishop, worshipped here on holiday 1933–44.'

He came to stay with friends, not far from the Gimbletts' farm. Often he wandered off on his own and said that was when he liked to compose some of his sermons. He got to know Harold well and stopped to talk cricket. 'Morning, Bish,' the young cricketer would say affectionately. When their son, Lawrence was born during the war, Harold and Rita were thrilled that Archbishop Temple blessed the baby.

On Feast days and harvest festivals, the Gimblett family monopolized their favourite pew under the window, in front of the pulpit. They sang heartily; shy Harold, with no ear for music, made the least noise.

I paused in the porch on my way out. There was a notice about the Samaritans and where to ring for help in Taunton and Bridgwater. The monthly newsletter carried a message for those who were despairing. They offered a poignant postscript to my mission.

Harold had left home for the first time at the age of eleven. He followed his two brothers to West Buckland. In his basically solitary way he was already a proficient rabbit-catcher. On his own shamefaced admission, Bicknoller's bird and cat population had decreased. And, clearly, once proud Somerset weather-cocks fluttered aloft in acute trepidation.

West Buckland School was founded on sound Christian principles in the mid nineteenth century. The parish rector of the time persuaded the second Earl Fortescue, Lord Lieutenant of Devon, to set up the kind of school that would provide education at a reasonable cost for children living in the county. The catchment area broadened after that, of course. There is Exmoor on one side and Dartmoor on the other, and the wind can whistle wickedly against the dormitory windows. It has never been a school for faint hearts. The spartan conditions today are the same as in the days when the Gimblett boys struggled with their Latin, and tried to keep warm at night. There is no heat in the dormitories and the temperatures in the winter are often below zero. West Buckland has no qualms about parading its philosophy of bringing boys up in a relatively tough school. 'There were times when we had to break the ice on the wash basins,' old boys tell you with pride in their eyes.

No one seemed to suffer. The boys kept warm on the rugby field and had fewer colds than most. They got on with their school work, struggled over one of the most rigorous cross-country courses in the country and, in the summer months, therapeutically helped local farmers with the haymaking. Harold was there in the Twenties; so was R. F. Delderfield, the journalist, novelist and playwright. His *To Serve Them All My Days* was set at West Buckland. It was the owlish, good-natured Ronnie Delderfield's sixth school and the one he liked best of all.

Young Harold tried to disguise his home-sickness when he first arrived. He lay awake at night. Term seemed an eternity and the new academic pressures and disciplines were not especially to

49

his liking. The school encouraged a feeling of community. He was not an easy mixer and was uncomfortably smothered by the exuberance of his form-mates: he missed those country lanes at Bicknoller and Stogumber where he could lose himself.

There were public school initiation ceremonies, not too unpleasant, to bear. He did his share of fagging. 'I fagged for a big chap called Gale, one of the honey family. I kept his rugger clothes clean, polished his boots and replaced his laces. Even took his boots off for him. But he was a nice chap. I used to get sweets and cakes as a reward.'

Tom Hitchins, later to become a governor and secretary of the Old Boys, was in the same house and form as Gimblett. He remembers him for his strong wrists. 'He told classmates he got them from carrying pig swill.' Harold 'Romeo' Boyer, a retired master from the school, was a prefect when Gimblett was in the middle school. 'He was a thick-set boy, a bit reticent certainly. Never distinguished in the academic sense. But soon to impress us all for his cricket.'

Sport came easily to young Gimblett. He walked into the Colts cricket XI and was soon made skipper. 'I scored my first 50 without really having to try,' he told me. There was no conceit in the voice. Wide-eyed fellow Colts forgot both their irregular verbs and their acne when this silent farmer's boy went in to bat. They reckoned that when he was a couple of years older, his impudent skiers would clear the hills altogether and land in the Bristol Channel.

Those pig-swilling wrists were made for hitting. What did colt cricketers care about finesse when Gimblett was winning matches for them without too much of it?

Paternal figures like 'Ned' Ross offered a word or two of gentle advice. But he knew this lad did not need too much coaching. He could hit straight – and that was a rare bonus. He had the exquisite timing from the outset: from the days he despatched rotting apples, bowled by brother Dennis, in the orchard at home, or when he lost the ball forever in Mr White's special match at Williton School.

Colts cricket, he found, was a way of expressing himself. He graduated to the 2nd XI by the age of twelve; and he was quickly introduced to the fledgeling ways of gamesmanship. The 2nd XI went off to play at Lynton and were plied with ice creams and pop before the match started. Such tuck-shop joys were too appealing to be resisted. 'We were also nobbled before the start when we went off to play at Dulverton. They gave us some rough cider. It went down beautifully with a generous helping of Exe salmon. We were too full to play well. The cider didn't help. I think we lost.'

Harold Gimblett generally had little time for personal records. A mention in Wisden never meant much to him. His record feats for Somerset, some of which may stand for ever, brought no more than a cursory glance when someone pointed them out in the Year Book. Conversely, he thinks he justified a line in the Guinness Book of Records.

Playing in an away 2nd XI fixture, he whacked the first ball he received into a clump of stinging nettles. 'Come on,' he yelled, as fielders danced involuntarily in pain and gingerly attempted to pick up the ball. By the time the ball was returned, and a bizarre line of fielders were applying dock leaves to their blisters, Gimblett had run seven.

His more sedate young partner played out the remainder of the over. Gimblett eyed the stinging nettles again and, with mischief in his heart, prepared for an improvised shot in that direction. His roguish ambition was excessive. He was out first ball. As he recalled it later: 'Just think of that. One ball. Seven runs. And out!'

The schoolboys enjoyed their sporting sorties into deepest Devon and Somerset. They savoured the surrealist stoppages of village cricket. Another favourite youthful memory of Harold is of the local G.P. who was batting for the opposition. Suddenly play was halted by an urgent call: someone near by had cut himself with a scythe. The doctor dropped his bat and ran from the wicket. He had left his medical bag in the pavilion; now he grabbed it and, without taking off his pads, tenderly laid the scythe victim on the grass and stitched his wound. The schoolboy cricketers left the field and gathered round in silent admiration.

51

They treated it as part of their education. Then the doctor washed his hands in the washing-up bowl, put on his batting gloves again and probably basked in a little collective adulation, nothing to do with cover drives, as he returned to the crease to continue a useful innings.

Nor did Gimblett ever forget a visit to Bridgetown in 1927. 'It was a postage stamp ground with the Exe running along one side. They used to pay someone a halfpenny to get the ball out of the river. There's a steepish hill on the ground and I remember hitting firmly up the hill. It would normally have been worth a boundary, so I called for 3. What I didn't realise was that the ball ran back down the hill to make it easy for the fielders. My partner was run out.'

He returned to that same quaint little ground many years afterwards. There was an old man sitting on the crude wooden bench. He was beaming and offered his hand. 'Hello, Harold. Dus thee remember, I bowled thee out on this hure ground a long time ago.' He had played against the boys from West Buckland. Gimblett, generally no lover of nostalgia, warmed to his friend. It was a happy and unlikely reunion.

Tears – and victory

By the time he was 13, Gimblett was in the school senior team, the youngest boy at West Buckland ever to manage it. Play took on a more competitive edge; opposing bowlers had more venom.

Against a touring United Banks side, he and his teammates visibly quaked as they saw the opening bowler marking out his run. It was the longest they had ever seen. He was at least ten years older, had a bellicose expression and a stubbly, lantern jaw rather like the post-war Freddie Trueman. The Demon Bowler pounded in and started to let them fly. Slender schoolboys, with innocent countenances and freshly creased flannels, were granted no favours. They were 30 for 7, impatient for once to return to their evening's prep in mid afternoon. Gimblett, newly promoted to the 1st team, walked timidly in at No. 9. Almost at once, the Banking Demon fired a lethal delivery. It got up and hit the boy with a sickening smack on the midriff. 'Down I went. I had a little cry and tried to brush the tears away as the fielders gathered round. I picked myself up, rubbed my tummy and, with the captain, Henry Pitts, I went on to win the game.'

It was a great moment for this shy schoolboy. Everyone at the school was watching. This almost unknown lad was the hero of West Buckland. The headmaster and senior masters said 'Well done, young Gimblett.' The other boys clapped him in. In confidential moments, during his county career, he would cite that triumph against the demons of the banking profession as one of his proudest cricketing memories: certainly on a par, in terms of self-satisfaction, with many of those centuries for Somerset.

His school batting was occasionally reckless, usually dominant. Privately, he was just as pleased with his off spinners and had a compulsive wish at all times to keep wicket.

When I was fifteen I was the only boy with his colours and I was automatically made captain. This terrified me. I knew I was the youngest member of the side. Now I'd be captaining the Head of the School, prefects and boys who were very much my senior academically. I was very worried indeed, so much so that I decided to see Sam Howells, Terror of the Lower School. You usually only visited his study once. You never went back a second time! I can still vividly picture him now, this ginger man with his pince-nez glasses. Somehow, I'd always escaped being sent to Sam. Now I bucked up courage to knock on his door. 'Can – can I have a talk with you, sir?' I blurted out. 'Strange, but I've been waiting for you. I thought you'd have been here before . . . what's it all about, then?'

'Sir, I just can't do this job of captaining the team. I'd like to get out of it.' – 'Don't be a fool, young Gimblett. Of course, you can do it. But I'll tell you what, I'll certainly be with you.' We talked for a long time, the Terror of the Lower School, the disciplinarian, and a boy who was really terrified of him.

It was, I think, the first intimation I had that I was a bit odd, a bit different from other boys.

Dear Sam, he became great friends with me. Whenever we played at home, he was there to give me support. I knew that he was behind me and that helped me a great deal. But eventually I lost Sam and I was on my own. That was when the mental battles really started . . . battles that continued right through my career. And only one person really knew anything about it. My wife.

He left school in 1931. By then his cricketing reputation had extended well beyond the West Buckland boundary. Somerset Stragglers, full of rather splendid chaps with a degree or two, business stature, polished accents and sporting prowess, invited him to play matches for them. In fact, they ensnared him with an opportunist nod from 'Ned' Ross, who had surveyed Harold's progress at West Buckland. By now the gaucherie of his early teenage years had largely passed: he had grown into a handsome, fair-haired lad, thicker still in the arms and shoulders, but well proportioned. He had an open-faced country boy's smile that was seen sparingly.

Friends noticed that the introvert youth was beginning to speak his mind, summoning up courage to express views and causing people to sit up. 'Ah well, these farming folk in West Somerset are an independent lot . . .' they'd say.

The Somerset Stragglers had a fixture with Wellington School in 1932. They were one short and 'Ned' had suggested bringing Gimblett into the side. 'He'll get a few runs for you – but I can't guarantee that he will get his head down for long,' he told the Stragglers' regulars. They warily put him down at No. 6.

Edward Ross, who must share some of the credit for Gimblett's subsequent fame, had given the Stragglers a canny assessment. On that sunny June afternoon, the newcomer showed no inclination at all to get his head down. He scored 142 in 75 minutes. It was his maiden century.

The shots were firm, sweet, audacious. They were made with

singular unconcern. His lofted straight drives carried fearless maturity. The Wellington schoolboys had never been taught to demonstrate such a disregard for the niceties of length and line. And, gallingly, he still only looked a schoolboy himself.

His own memories of that first hundred are joyful – and saucy – ones. 'The Wellington headmaster was sitting near the pavilion having a nap and I whacked one which bounced up and rattled against the woodwork of the deckchair. He jumped up, charged on to the field and pulled up a stump. As far as I can remember, he gave one of the boys six of the best for no reason at all.'

But in the previous August, just after leaving school for the last time, he had played for Watchet against Wellington, the town side, not the school. Wellington batted first and scored 160; Watchet, the home team, blown away – at least psychologically – on the breeziest of all Somerset grounds, were very soon 37 for 7. Then two teenagers, Gimblett and Alan Pearse, himself later to play for Somerset, came together. It developed into a stand that club members continue to talk about and pretend, in most cases, that they witnessed. Gimblett made 91 and Pearse 33 without being parted, to win the match. They did it against fine club bowling. Gimblett himself was much taken with a Wellington bowler called Page, 'the fastest I had ever come up against . . . I got rather partial to pace bowling after that.'

In 1933, Gimblett found himself playing for Watchet against the Stragglers and was again in extraordinary form. He made 150 in 80 minutes, as if in a hurry to get home for the milking (one of many agricultural chores that, in truth, did not appeal at all to him).

That windswept Watchet ground, with its docks just over the boundary and a line of evergreens deliberately planted to act as breakers, has seen some great innings. Young Gimblett's, against the Stragglers, was surely the most murderous. Fielders had repeatedly to jump the wall into the distant road to retrieve the ball. The Stragglers' despairing and then haphazard pattern of bowling changes was made to look risible in the extreme.

Then came an incident that took everyone by surprise. Gimblett reached 150 and suddenly started to walk back to the pavilion. One of the senior members of the fielding side, with red face and toffee accent, grasped the significance of what was happening. No one retired undefeated against Somerset Stragglers. It just wasn't done, dammit.

'I say, look here, Gimblett, you can't simply leave when you've scored 150, old chap.'

The young batsman looked at his accuser, more concerned with etiquette than bestowing praise. He turned without a word and returned to the wicket. He walked down the pitch to the next ball, deliberately missed it and was stumped.

You didn't tell a Gimblett what to do.

Cricket for Williton, briefly, or Watchet was all very well. But what of a career? On an uncle's and brother Dennis's advice, Harold went off to sample the grocery trade in London. It was, he found out, 'pen pushing and seventeen bob a week'. London however, was a revelation to him after the sparsely populated rolling hills of Somerset and Devon. For relaxation he played rugby at weekends, although he had always been a useful soccer forward. After rugger for the Y.M.C.A. he eagerly returned to Lyons in Tottenham Court Road for high tea – and then off to the sixpenny queue at the Dominion nearby. This was where he listened to Jack Payne and his Band. There, too, he laughed at a Liverpudlian comedian called Ted Ray. Years later, with an endearingly naive touch, he met the stand-up comic. 'Do you remember me, Ted? I used to go along regularly to watch you with your violin at the Dominion.'

When it came to summer time, Harold played some cricket for London Devonians. There were other lads, including Dennis, from West Buckland in the side. He made plenty of runs but began to long for the open spaces and village cricket again. Impulsively he wrote to his father. 'I've given it a go and I don't like it, Dad. Can I come home?'

The father, with some parental pleasure we imagine, replied: 'There are 10,000 jobs waiting for you here, son.'

If Harold inherited any marked enthusiasm for the farming

56

industry, it never really surfaced. He cleaned out the stalls and fed the pigs. But there was not the remotest possibility in his mind that he would follow his father and grandfather into a permanent life on the farm. His biceps were right for it: not his hands, and certainly not his mind. He began fancifully to think about joining the Black Watch or the police force until he realised he was not tall enough for either. When he called on a firm of electrical engineers, who had a garage in Taunton, they told him bluntly that they had no vacancies. Hadn't he heard of the Depression? So for the time being, he stayed at Blakes Farm. His head, as his tolerant father discovered, was by now full of cricket.

He started playing for Watchet up to three times a week. Mr Gimblett, to his eternal credit, did not dissuade him. He took over Harold's chores, even at haymaking time. The son had some guilt about the arrangement but not to the extent of rectifying the disproportionate amount of honest-to-goodness labour by other members of the family. A few pointed words were at times passed between the brothers.

Harold stayed with Watchet C.C. for four seasons and took his turn, with all the others, in cutting and rolling the pitch. He seldom missed a match – or net practice on a Tuesday night. The club facilities were good and the seven-mile round trip on his old cycle never bothered him. When he scored a second century at the expense of the Somerset Stragglers, the local newspaper reporters began sharpening their pencils. They regularly noted his propensity for high scores, compiled at indecent speed.

Today the walls of the Watchet C.C. clubhouse are filled with team photographs. The surprisingly boyish Gimblett seems to be on many of them. There is a framed letter from the then sports editor of the *Manchester Evening News*, complimenting the club on the dynamic progress of one of its members. The letter is dated 1936: Gimblett had just scored a marvellous 93 and 160 not out, in only his second season of county cricket, against Lancashire at Old Trafford. Every fraying photograph on that pavilion wall is an eloquent essay on its own. There is Gimblett, jauntily in action in the nets; Gimblett with Watchet colleague Alan Pearse, on the

June day in 1936 when it was Pearse's turn to make his debut for Somerset at Frome.

By this time, young Gimblett's mentor was W. G. Penny, a master tailor who once employed a dozen men at his Watchet premises. Everyone knew W.G. For 49 years he was the secretary of the Cricket Club; he guided it with efficiency and good humour. He was a Gladstonian Liberal and an equally good Methodist. His passion for matters political and Godly was extended to cricket. He loved Watchet C.C. and, of course, Somerset. For several years he had encouraged and cajoled Gimblett; intuitively, he knew that the boy had quite exceptional talent and must play for his county, if not country. More than anyone else, W.G. had the perspicacity to ensure that Gimblett would not slip out of Somerset's grasp. By sheer cussed insistence and undaunted perseverence, he guided Harold to the Taunton county ground.

Gimblett, for his part, was grateful to W.G. though he was at times embarrassed and even irritated by the course being determined for him. Hardly once – and this is confirmed by W.G.'s son, Bromley, himself an ageless supporter of cricket as club player and county committee man – did Gimblett express the slightest wish to play for Somerset.

W.G. was apparently an opportunist businessman as well as an excellent tailor. 'Never once did he watch a match,' claimed Gimblett to me, 'without selling a suit of clothes.' I am sure there was affectionate exaggeration in the story, as in another memory from the days of the early Thirties. 'A hefty member of the Somerset Stragglers bent down to field the ball and his trousers split. In no time at all, W.G. was out on the field with his tape measure.' It was often said that one of Mr Penny's unfulfilled ambitions was to make Harold a suit of clothes. 'For some reason, I wouldn't let him. I regretted it later, when it was too late.'

Everyone nominated W.G.'s resourcefulness among his shining qualities. He turned up for the first F.A. cup final at Wembley without a ticket. West Country friends told him he was mad to try to get in. Mr Penny, who naturally cut a neat, dignified appearance, put on his best black bowler and walked into the Stadium immediately after the Royal Family. He was mistaken for a personal detective.

Perhaps he needed even greater ingenuity occasionally, back at the Watchet ground, to nurse the capricious Gimblett temperament. Harold would go into his shell for no reason at all. He would give his wicket away, simply because 'he wasn't feeling up to scratch'. Mostly he enjoyed his matches for Watchet. He relished the romantic and eccentric canvas of what, in spirit, was the Village Game.

We were playing Wiveliscombe, I remember, and the bus broke down on the way. We arrived at the ground at a quarter to five. It was the bus that did 'the cinema round' for the local villages to Minehead. Because of its commitments, we knew that only two hours and twenty minutes' play would be possible. The two teams decided to take tea while the shortened game was going on. 'Wivvy' batted first and rather cheated. They batted for one hour twenty minutes. That didn't leave us long. I went in first and Tommy Thorn came on to bowl. I got 30 in the first over – and we just kept going. We caught the bus with time to spare.

And there was another match, where the home team had a well-known combination – father and son. Dad was the umpire and son did the bowling. They also had a vicar in the side so the Watchet boys had to watch their language. It was a dull day and the light got steadily worse. By the time it was our turn to bat there was hardly any light at all. Alan Pearse went in first with me and he knew of the umpire's reputation. 'If you give anyone out, I'll crown you,' he said. Whenever we hit the ball we started running – we couldn't see where the ball had gone. It came to the last over and we still needed 28. The vicar was bowling and I hit him four times across the road, up among the pigs. That was four sixes – and I finished the twilight match with a four. Sorry, vicar.

We are drawn to the conclusion that Gimblett was so much happier in these carefree matches than when he played at Lord's, the Oval or Leeds.

It was during his days with Watchet that he met Marguerita Burgess. The first time he saw her he was waiting at The Cross for the bus, and she walked past. She made such an impression that, years later, he was able to give a precise description of her appearance. She was wearing a brown beret and had her hair in a pigtail. His romantic attachments up to then had been few but he turned to a teammate and said: 'She's worth catching.' The reply was that she was Fred Burgess's daughter and was probably a bit particular with whom she went out.

In fact, the unlikely friendship ripened – in a very proper, conventional way. When he pedalled home along New Road after cricket practice, a mile from Rita's home in Knapp House, he flashed his cycle lamp in the direction of her bedroom. She took a renewed interest in cricket. But she unwisely allowed her attention to lapse one Saturday afternoon as she sat with her mother near the Watchet pavilion. Harold was batting at the time and Rita wonders whether he noticed that she was reading a paper. He hit the ball in her direction and it went straight through the newspaper. 'Missed my head by inches,' she jokes with retrospective comfort.

Bromley Penny, who served on the county's executive committee and was chairman of the finance committee for a number of years after he had finished tossing up his leg breaks for Watchet, remembers vividly the annual matches before the war when a county side arrived to play W. G. Penny's XI. It was an all-day fixture and the club president, the late Edgar Reed, footed the bill for lunch at the West Somerset Hotel. 'For some reason I had to put pressure on Harold several times to play. It was pointed out to him that he was my father's protégé, after all.'

Gimblett's reluctance to take part in those special matches can be interpreted in various ways. I don't believe he was being cussed or arrogant. Much more likely, he was afraid of failing publicly in front of established county cricketers. The young buccaneer's bravado was deceptive. He preferred not to be tested at the higher level.

It is probably true that one or two of the Somerset amateurs –

and, maybe, cynical pros – sniffed at his uninhibited approach. They don't like village upstarts to start driving them off the front foot, without a care about seam or swing. His record in the W. G. Penny XI games was, in fact, much to the liking of the Watchet intimates. 'I actually came up against Jack White for the first time in one of these annual fixtures,' Gimblett said. 'He was the Somerset captain and I hit him for three enormous sixes. I got 61 that day and was on top of the world.'

We don't know what J. C. White made of that. By nature he was a man of few words: he disguised his emotions. Perhaps he said in that slow, deliberate delivery of his: 'Ah well, he must be all right – he comes from my part of Somerset. And we're both farming folk.'

When Harold thumped Jack White's flighted left-arm slows miles out of the ground, oblivious to the fact that the wily bowler played for England, the older Mr Penny looked at his friends and winked. 'I'll have this lad in the Somerset team before long,' he promised.

It was not as easy as that. The county did not share W.G.'s ecstatic faith. They dismissed the young player as too flash. It was one thing to swing the bat at every other ball on a village green. Gimblett, they argued in their remote and prejudiced manner, had neither the technique nor the temperament to make real progress in the game.

Good-natured club members in Watchet claimed that tailor Penny spent almost as much time advocating a county trial for Gimblett as he did measuring for suits of clothes. He persuaded Somerset's senior professional Tom Young, that frail, underrated all-rounder, to take a look. Young's verdict, reflecting the caution of other county officials, was: 'I'm not sure he's quite good enough.'

That was not going to deter W.G. He continued to pepper the county headquarters with fulsome recommendations. And at last Somerset, more irked by the mentor's persistence than fired by excitement over Gimblett's innate and pugnacious skills with a bat, agreed to a fortnight's trial.

He arrived at the county ground in the May of 1935. He had no cricket bag and only a discoloured bat which looked as though it had seen plenty of fours at West Buckland, if not squashed apples in the Bicknoller orchard before that. He was shown the way to the professionals' dingy dressing room. There they were, all six of them – Arthur Wellard, Bill Andrews, the Lee brothers, Frank and Jack, and Horace Hazell. Heroes all.

Someone said: 'There's two pegs. That's where you change. And speak when you're spoken to.' It may sound brutal but it was the best advice I was ever given . . . I didn't know anything about cricket at that level, so why should I be able to pass judgement? The advice was given in a kindly way.

I came out changed and Arthur said: 'At least you *look* like a cricketer. We'll soon find out if you are one.' We went to the nets. Wellard and Andrews started knocking over the stumps faster than I could pick them up. I realized for the first time the enormous gap between first class and club cricket.

Somerset went off to play Surrey, I think. John Daniell came up to me and said: 'You may as well finish the week. We'll pay you 35 shillings and your bus fare. Afraid you're just not good enough.' My immediate reaction wasn't one of disappointment. 'This has been one of the most wonderful weeks of my life, sir. I've met all my heroes.'

I helped to pick up the grass and to prepare the wicket for the next match. And I ended up as 12th man for both sides. I got a couple of quid for that and felt like a millionaire. Somerset then had another away match and I helped once more on the ground. I'd given up any thought at all of playing for Somerset by this time.

I was about to catch the bus and head for home on the Friday night when news came through that Laurie Hawkins had got a knock on the thumb and couldn't play on the Saturday. Somerset were down to ten men. There was no one else available. That was the county in those days. J. C. White apparently said: 'We'll just have to play this bloke, Gimblett.

He won't give anything away in the field and it'll keep old Billy Penny quiet!'

That was how it happened. Gimblett's view, as expressed above, clearly mellowed. Mr Daniell's rejection was rather more blunt; the player's response, once it had sunk in, was not without resentment. As for W.G., his amiable Wesleyan principles were sorely stretched. He was angry when he heard that Somerset had taken no more than a perfunctory look before discreetly pointing back towards Bicknoller. Bromley says: 'It did upset Dad a great deal. I remember he went as red as a carrot when he heard.' He offered, in fact, to pay a week's wages himself, for Harold to stay on at the county ground.

'He's not the kind of player to judge in the nets. They restrict him. Give him a game to prove himself.'

And then suddenly, Hawkins was out and the rejected Gimblett was in. The rest of the county team were travelling back from an away match. The county ground was almost deserted on a Friday afternoon. There were one or two muttered words of congratulations. It was seen as something of an embarrassment.

That evening Harold went out with Rita. Reticently he told her that he was to play for Somerset against Essex at Frome the following day.

They were two shy lovers and neither was demonstrative. But Rita impulsively gave Harold a kiss. 'It was a kind of good-luck kiss. He was taken back but I could see that he liked it. He grinned at me and said he would be all right now.'

So he was. Spurred by a girl friend's kisses and with a borrowed bat in his hands, he walked out to score one of the most romantic and publicized maiden centuries in the history of English first class cricket.

THE CRICKETER

Fiction at Frome

West Country schoolboys came to recite the facts and circumstances of Gimblett's magnificent and impudent century of 18th May 1935 with a vocal vigour never remotely matched in the ritual of the twice-times table. It almost became part of the required curriculum.

The century belonged to fiction. The plot was altogether too thrillingly fashioned: a confectioned scenario that mocked credulity. It came from the genre of sporting stories of excessive heroism on the field, written by Victorian and Edwardian clergy, warmed by their imagination as they sat in draughty rectories. Young readers enjoyed but did not need to believe. It was all part of the romance of cricket.

Yet it did happen, at Frome. A village lad from the Quantocks, turned down by his county, was suddenly asked to play because no one else could be found to make up the eleven. For once, not even an extra from Somerset's intermittent band of strolling players, amateurs who appeared from abroad or the pages of Debrett for a jolly game or two between country house parties, could be spirited up at such short notice. So there was John Daniell saying, without too much conviction: 'Do you know where Frome is, young Gimblett? Can you get there on your own?'

Harold was not too sure that he could. He stammered that

perhaps he could catch one very early bus to Bridgwater, and then another to Frome. The secretary pondered the geographical complications. 'You'll never arrive on time that way. Get to Bridgwater by nine o'clock and I'll ask Luckes to pick you up in his car.'

Few centuries have been documented with more detail and loving labour. There have been embellishments at a few thousand cricket dinners since then. The commas and the colour of Harold's pocket handkerchief may have varied slightly, but never the joyful spirit of the day's theatre.

It was a dynamic piece of fledgeling cricket by a player so unknown that the scorecard could give no initials for him. Yet his reputation was to be established forever, by what happened on that bitterly cold May afternoon at Frome, where the tents billowed noisily as they do at an early Spring point-to-point. White railings encircled the small playing area, adding to the hint of a rural racing scene.

Frome was proud of its one county match a season. The town had a small population but a lively and loyal support for Somerset cricket. Facilities on the ground were modest, with plenty of functional corrugated iron, and wooden benches transported in for the occasion. There was no room on the scoreboard for individual innings. The voices around the boundary were pure, throaty Somerset: but different from Taunton, Weston or Yeovil. And different from Bicknoller.

On his cassettes, Gimblett talked ramblingly of many things. He chose to give only a brief, factual account of his century at Frome. It occupied just a minute of reminiscence. The dismissive attitude was part of him and we shall return to it. Mrs Gimblett told me: 'I kept the cuttings. Harold would have destroyed them.'

It would be quite wrong for me also to dismiss his maiden innings for Somerset, although in the ways of folklore, everyone will know that he was up well before 6 a.m. on that Saturday morning and narrowly missed the bus to Bridgwater. The next bus was in two hours' time.

He had a little all-purpose bag within which – you would never have guessed – was his own bruised and discoloured bat and a few sandwiches considerately dropped in by his mother. Maternal kindness had also ensured freshly creased flannels and a clean shirt. He stood, a forlorn figure, on the narrow country road and wondered what he should do now. He started walking, vaguely in the direction of Bridgwater, and then heard a lorry from behind. Harold thumbed it down, something he had never done before. The dialogue that followed had an endearing quality to it.

'Sorry, I've just missed the bus.'

'OK, jump in. Where are you going?'

'To Frome.'

'Why?'

'To play cricket.'

'Who for?'

'Somerset.'

'Oh, ah!'

The lorry driver did not believe Gimblett. How could he have? On his own admission, Harold looked like a wide-eyed innocent, in trouble because he was late for work.

Wally Luckes was waiting for him at Bridgwater and they reached the ground in good time. Some supporters were already in their place. They recognized the little wicket keeper and offered a cheery greeting. No one recognized Gimblett.

Then I met the Essex players. Jack O'Connor . . . Laurie Eastman . . . Maurice Nichols . . . Ray and Peter Smith . . . Tommy Wade, Tom Pearce . . . I realized I was scared stiff. Wally Luckes gave me the only bit of advice. 'Peter Smith will always bowl you a googlie so be ready for it.' I didn't even know what a googlie was – I'd never seen one. Wally patiently explained that it looked like a leg spinner but went the other way.

Reggie Ingle was the Somerset captain and he put Gimblett at No. 8. He won the toss and was soon regretting it. Nichols was using all his natural speed, as well as a biting wind that was

66

sweeping across the ground. Jack Lee, Ingle and White were all caught at slip and Somerset were 35 for 3. You could hear the groans around the boundary. By lunch, Frank Lee and C. C. C. (Box) Case were also out and the score was 105 for 5.

The Bath amateur, H. D. Burrough quickly followed. At 2.20 p.m. 20-year-old Harold Gimblett, head down and already pessimistic about what he imagined was a token appearance in county cricket, meandered to the wicket to join Wellard. Someone in the crowd shouted: 'Leave it to Arthur, son.'

During the lunch interval, Wellard had put a friendly hand on Gimblett's shoulder. 'Don't think much of your bat, cock. Why don't you borrow my spare one?' And so he did.

Peter Smith sniffed a novice. His third ball to Gimblett was a googlie. The young batsman had not spotted it but he pushed it away to mid wicket and was off the mark. In his second over from Smith, Gimblett straight-drove to the boundary. That felt good. The Frome supporters rather approved of the way he did that. Who was this lad? Gimb-Gimblett or something? Wasn't he the lad who was always whacking sixes in village matches?

The likeable Peter Smith chuckled silently to himself. He summoned up additional wiles. But so much for cunning. His fourth over after lunch cost 15 runs, all of them to Gimblett. When the leg break was fractionally over-pitched, the young batsman put his left foot down and heaved the spinning ball over mid off for six. It landed on the top of the beer tent, a marquee temporarily deserted as the rubicund drinkers moved outside to savour this jaunty newcomer.

Gimblett suddenly realized he was enjoying himself. Nichols was by far the fastest bowler he had ever met but the young batsman had the clear eyes and nimble feet to keep him out of trouble. In nine overs, Somerset added 69 runs; 48 of them came from Gimblett. He was actually outscoring Wellard, and not many managed that. The ever-bronzed Arthur, jangling the loose change in his flannel trousers, ready for the next poker school, only smiled.

The half-century came with a six. It had taken 28 minutes and he had received 33 balls. By now the spectators had shed their reserve: they were cheering every shot. The beer was left undrunk.

Wellard miscalculated an off break from Vic Evans and was stumped. But then came his look-alike and inseparable mate, Andrews. In between, Luckes had been bowled by Nichols, back with the new ball.

New ball? You couldn't afford such niceties around the village greens of West Somerset. Gimblett threshed his way on, swinging and sweeping and driving whenever he could. There was hardly a false shot. Essex fielders rued the short boundary; they were generous enough to applaud some of the sixes.

Nichols dug one in short and the Somerset No. 8, with ludicrous time to spare, hooked it for four. Then, oblivious to pace, Gimblett took two more runs through the covers.

He had no idea how many he had scored; the scoreboard gave the minimum of information. But the spectators soon told him. The cover drive had brought him his century. It had been scored out of 130 and had taken 63 minutes. As the fastest hundred of the season it earned him the Lawrence Trophy.

It was, I suppose, one of those days you dream of. I can't work it out. I took all the praise but Bill Andrews, who got 71, was even faster in his scoring. I savoured the moment – but loathed the publicity that followed.

Gimblett gave a simple return catch when he had scored 123 in 79 minutes. Nichols still returned a splendid 6–87 in 23 overs. Peter Smith finished with 1–89 in 13 overs and must have been particularly wary when bowling to low-order newcomers after that. Essex never recovered from such an unceremonious mauling. They were bowled out for 141 and 147. The late Jack Lee took four wickets in their first innings and five in their second.

Fleet Street was engaged at that time in a circulation battle of ruthless proportions. Pop journalism carried with it gimmicks and ballyhoo in the bid for new readers. Gimblett's triumph had immense human interest. The photographers and the feature

68

writers turned up at the farm. He posed reluctantly and hated the whole thing.

In a newspaper article, Jack Hobbs congratulated Harold but tempered his compliments by saying it left the young Somerset batsman with a reputation he might have difficulty sustaining. Gimblett knew that only too well.

He played 15 more matches in 1935; that in itself is something of an achievement for an unenthusiastic trialist given his cards before the season even started. He ended up with 482 runs and an average of 17.

His muscles, not used to the demands of three-day cricket, took a few strains and he missed several games through injury. There were also problems with his technique. He went through a wretched spell in July when, in five matches, his highest score was 18, at Clacton. There were demoralizing ducks at Bath, against the South Africans, at Pontypridd and Wells. He would lie in bed at night and say to himself: 'They are finding me out. That John Daniell was right – I'm not good enough.'

Following the artificial euphoria of Frome, he was kept in the team for the visit to Lord's – but only because of R. J. O. Meyer's malaria. The ritual of the Long Room made no great impression on him. From the start he disliked the M.C.C.'s haughtier elements. His first appearance at Lord's brought him a 50 in the second innings and, of more lasting joy, a meeting with Patsy Hendren.

> I had pulled a muscle and had come off the field. In the professionals' room we used to have to sit on a table to look out of the window – that's what they thought of us. There I was, looking very forlorn, I've no doubt, when who should come and join me but the one and only Patsy Hendren . . . the most lovable and ugly man there ever was. He talked to me for the whole afternoon. I was in another world. It was a wonderful experience.

Gimblett made his half-century with the help of a runner. He returned to the side to play against Kent at Taunton in late June.

At the crease he sparred and missed. Wiseacres in the members' enclosure looked at each other in eloquent silence. There had been murmurings about his wanton disregard for the basic requirements of defensive batting. The Gimblett approach showed a worrying imbalance that was bound to work against him as experienced county bowlers sensed his flaws.

There is a popular myth that he was given a trial with Somerset on the strength of his bowling. He was a useful and accurate schoolboy and Watchet club bowler but, at the Taunton nets, he seemed capable merely of pitching on a reasonable length. Mr Ingle therefore surprised him by suddenly calling him into the attack against Kent. At modest medium-pace, he bowled half a dozen encouragingly tight overs for 6–2–13–2. No self-respecting gentle seamer would feel ashamed of those figures on his bowling debut, especially as the first victim was Leslie Ames. The ball seamed delicately, deceived Ames and Luckes took the catch.

In the second innings he took another wicket. 'You bowl a bit as well then, cock,' said Wellard, his mouth creasing in a kindly smile. When he came to Bath for the next match, against Gloucestershire, Gimblett returned what were to prove the best bowling figures of his career, a rather remarkable 4.1–0–10–4.

The caprices of the Bath wicket are well known, of course. Such mischief, on the part of the pitch, always seems to me that shade more unbecoming on a ground bordered by sedate Georgian architecture and ecclesiastical propriety. I missed Buse's calamitous benefit match; but I was there when Brian Langford, still a boy, rolled the stumps over with his leisurely off spinners to take 14–156 in the next fixture. And I saw Somerset beat the Australians for the first time, at Bath, by seven wickets in 1977.

In the same way, Bath befriended Gimblett in the match with Gloucestershire in 1935. The West Country rivals have felicitiously produced many taut finishes. That one ended with Somerset winning by one wicket. At 102–6 in their second innings, Gloucestershire were intent on building a fragile innings. They knew the wicket would get no easier. Gimblett was known to them as a young batsman whose maiden century was a fluke; they did not even realize that he occasionally bowled, too. And they were surprised when he was brought up from the outfield to partner Andrews (6–38).

He almost immediately bowled Billy Neale, the visiting county's top scorer. Monty Cranfield, remembered in Bristol as both an efficient practical joker and off spinner who spent too long in the shadows of Tom Goddard, was quickly lbw. to Gimblett; and Charlie Parker, no doubt with a few audible curses, gave a return catch. Vic Hopkins, a Gloucestershire wicket keeper, sandwiched between Harry Smith and Andy Wilson, was the fourth victim. Tailenders, perhaps, but the innings was suddenly all over for 126: and Gimblett was in danger of being called an all-rounder.

His trial had obviously been extended. He found county cricket a strange new life. It was never easy for him to integrate with the rest of the pros on away matches. They slapped him on the back, told good-natured jokes at his expense and pulled him into the occasional game of cards. He was wise enough, after noting Wellard's uncanny knack of memorizing nearly every card in the pack, to decline most invitations to join the poker school. He was already learning from the masters of the trade how to make a few bob on his expenses. He saw no point in handing it over towards the likeable Arthur's next flash sports coat.

Somerset went off to Maidstone at the end of July. Gimblett loved the atmosphere of the Festival week; he also had reason to be grateful to Leslie Ames.

Tich Freeman was bowling. I played forward and missed completely – I simply didn't know which way the ball was going. If Les had waited one half-second, he could have had the bails off as I lost my balance. But Les, God bless him, whispered to me: 'It's all right, Harold, I've thrown it back.' That was the camaraderie of cricket then. I only wish it was played like that today. I went on to get 61 and Frank Lee got some useful runs. And we won the match.

Then it was back to the Weston Festival. I dropped a catch

and was given a rocket by Jack White. He was a hard man. The trouble was the catch was off his bowling. He didn't drop so many himself when he was bowling!

The third match at Clarence Park was against Notts. That was when I met Harold Larwood, by then not quite the force he had been – but still a bit quick, I can tell you. I watched him sideways on. It looked so easy. He had that beautiful rhythm. Then it was my turn, at No. 9. For the first ball, I was still lifting my bat up when the delivery was on its way to fine leg for 2. The second ball hit me in the box and laid me out. I eventually got to my feet and prepared for Larwood's third ball. This illustrates what a great batsman I was to become. I cleverly got my bat out of the way in good time – and away went my off stump!

When I next came up against him, he let one go and hit me in the ribs. I had absolutely no time to move. I went down on one knee and he asked if I was all right. 'Can I call you Lol?' I asked. 'Sure,' he said sympathetically. 'Well, make me one promise, Lol. Not in the same place again,' I implored, rubbing my ribs. He grinned. And he never bounced one at me again.

Bill Voce was the one I found difficult to play. He was left-arm quick, round the wicket. That meant pitching about off stump and coming at you all the time. After about an hour it got painful. Joe Hardstaff was one of the sharks fielding just round the corner. I turned to him and said: 'Blow this lark, I'm not sticking this.' Very quietly, he said to me: 'Take a new guard. Take off stump.' I did – and from that moment, Bill Voce held no terrors for me. Just after, I remember, he dropped one short at me. I was in the right position and I smashed a car windscreen with a six. Joe Hardstaff and I became good friends.

I'd taken quite a battering from Larwood and Voce. But there was also Harold Butler, and Arthur Staples wasn't so slow. The knuckles on my hand were sore. I came into the dressing room and looked in the mirror. I was decidedly grey.

Then a small, stocky man came up and, without saying anything, picked up my bat from my bag and gave it a whirl. He walked out, still without a word. 'Who's that?' I asked Wally

72

Luckes. 'The great George Gunn.' 'Blimey, I'd love to meet him.' 'You will!'

Next morning George Gunn approached me in the dressing room before the game. 'I've got a couple of bats for you with the compliments of the firm.' I picked them up. 'But Mr Gunn, they're too heavy.' He looked at me. 'Listen, son, if I give you a six-inch nail, which are you going to use for it – a little hammer or a big hammer? The big one, of course. Now when you go in to bat first, those balls come at you at a great speed. You need something big to stop them and make them go on their way. These bats have been specially made for you this morning.' I bucked up courage. 'Mr Gunn, what weight did you use?' He told me three pounds and I found it hard to believe. I was taken downstairs on one occasion at Trent Bridge and one of George's bats was taken out of its case. It was three pounds in weight. I went out to make 94 in the second innings and never felt a thing.

But we are already moving into 1936 and that is premature. First there was a contract – a proper one – to think of. Whatever the sways of the pendulum in Gimblett's first season, the demeanour at times of almost indifference and the self-doubts, he had earned extended wages on a more official basis. 'Somerset offered me a real professional contract, much to the horror of at least one member of the family. Ah well, he was a bit of a snob.' Up to then Gimblett had been paid by the match. Now he was being promised £300 if he played in all the matches – 'and for this princely sum the pros played their hearts out to win. We didn't very often go after a draw, and then usually because the captains weren't very good friends.'

He signed the contract and went home to the farm to do, as he put it, some serious thinking. In his private way he liked all the other pros: and now he was one of them. He warmed less to the amateurs.

That winter, as he began to worry about the approaching 1936 season, he frequently thought of Jack Lee's words to him: 'Don't you bother yourself, Harold, about them going out of a different gate. Just you think that we're good enough in our own right to be playing this game and getting paid for it. All the amateurs have to do is put on a pretty hat.'

With a few obvious exceptions, Gimblett's initial impression of the Somerset amateurs was one of muted enthusiasm. He disliked the snobberies of the first class game and magnified them in his head. He had never really taken to the Quantocks gentry and told friends he was a Liberal. It was said that over the Mendips at Bristol, Charlie Parker even cussed the amateurs when they put down his catches. A young professional, Charlie Barnett, product of a minor public school, eloquently stood his ground. Gimblett liked the sound of that.

'Go off and play cricket'

In the March of 1936, at lambing time, Harold's father died. Percy was a strong man, six foot and sixteen stone. It was a family claim that father could put his shoulder under the back end of a horse and lift it off the ground. He would get up at six o'clock, light his pipe and put the kettle on to make a cup of tea. That was also what he was doing at 11 a.m. when he suddenly keeled over. Lewis snatched at him or he would have fallen into the fire. He had suffered a stroke and was dead within a week. Harold, who took his turn at the all-night vigil at lambing time, was on hand when his father collapsed. He was distraught.

'Dad was a good farmer. In 1923 he'd put the whole farm into wheat. The crop was flattened. It was a gamble and he lost what was an awful lot of money for those days.'

After the funeral, the family solicitor chatted to the family and then turned to Harold. 'You go off and play cricket – the farm can't carry both you and Lewis.' That at least was one problem solved; young Gimblett's career was determined for him.

To keep fit he played a few games of football for Watchet. Arthur Langdon, later the council chairman, kept goal – and did it well enough for an unlikely Leeds United scout to take a look at him. George Alexander was a tough centre forward who, according to Gimblett, had the knack of tripping himself up to win regular penalties for his team. Harold was played on the left wing but he was not quite sure why. He had no left foot shot and used to have to swivel back on to his right to centre. A Dulverton opponent once baited him about his non-existent left foot. 'He got me going and I scored a marvellous goal with my left. Never did it again. I astonished myself more than him.'

But soccer was only a Saturday-afternoon way of marking time. He missed the sixes and the subtlety of cricket.

Back at the county ground in April for the pre-season nets, he was greeted by little knots of Taunton bystanders. 'Gi' us a hundred in yer fuss game, Harold – like you did last yurr.' Everyone expected too much, he told himself. Bertie Bisgood from Glastonbury had hit a century on his maiden appearance for Somerset in 1907 and no one had made such an almighty fuss of that.

At the end of nets, Gimblett walked across the field. He sniffed the freshly cut grass and surveyed the ground's especial intimacies. He reckoned he could hook into St James' churchyard or clear the lofty press box for a straight drive on to the roof of the secretary's office. The prospect amused him.

Then the greenhorn frowned as he contemplated the season ahead. 'They'll find me out,' he kept repeating to himself. The realities of 1936 were astonishing. He scored 1,608 runs and five centuries. And, even more amazingly, he played twice for England in only his second season of county cricket. Headline writers were waxing lyrical; every spunky second former was claiming, as he went out to bat in his house match, that he was Gimblett.

The Indians came for the opening match in May and Harold, very much to his surprise, found himself at No. 2. He scored a century in the first innings and an undefeated 46 in the second. The Tourists shivered under their sweaters; they also quivered as this inexperienced opener went after that. The Wisden writer – and we should overlook any shred of understandable partiality in the account – said: 'Those who saw him score 149 for once out, by almost perfect coordination of eye, hand and foot were practically convinced that Somerset need look no further for an opening partner for Frank Lee.'

But wait: in no time he had an average of more than 200. He travelled up to Old Trafford for the second match to score 93 and 160 not out. It was a magnificent feat. Neville Cardus, who could talk as well as he could write, singled the young Somerset batsman out for a chat. 'His lovely two-column write-up was one I proudly kept . . . It was one of the moments in life to be treasured.' For a long time after that, Gimblett's picture was displayed in the Old Trafford pavilion, with its scribbled note from Cardus, saying in effect: 'Thanks for sending us this young player.' Perhaps it is still there.

I also met George Duckworth, Jack Iddon and the others. I heard George's famous appeal, a bit like a seagull, very high-pitched. He tried very hard to get me out in the last over before lunch in the first innings. There were three appeals in four balls. The fifth delivery was well outside the off stump. I really let it go and it was in his hands when I went through the motions of a late cut. As he appealed I spun round and pinned his hands to the ground with the end of my bat. He swore and I don't blame him – it must have hurt a bit. I said: 'Come on, George, cut out this flippin' drama. You know I'm not likely to touch them as wide as that. When I get a touch, then you can shout.' During the afternoon I went fast asleep and was bowled by Booth for 93. It was a straight one and I played all round it. I returned to the pavilion and the members stood as I came up the steps to the dressing room. Here was tradition at its absolute best. I couldn't have spoken. There were tears in my eyes.

In the second innings I played right through the day, the last 45 minutes with Horace. Off the fifth ball I'd push for a single. We worked it out to a fine art. We saved the game and Lancashire claimed the extra half-hour in vain. The Manchester–London express was held up for us. Think of that – delayed for two professional cricketers from the West Country. We were rushed by taxi, pads still on and bats in our hand, along with our scorer, to the station. Railway staff ushered us into our reserved compartment. Again the Old Trafford members had risen to us. It was glorious moment to cherish.

The same engaging combination, Gimblett and Hazell, power and podge, was soon in evidence again. A week later Somerset were at Kettering. There was no play on the Saturday and Somerset then enforced the follow-on. The young opener was told, superfluously, that he could give it a belt. His instinctive response was to score a century before lunch on the Monday. There were six sixes and nine fours; 72 of his runs came in fifteen strokes. It would be churlish indeed to dwell on the chance he gave when he was 90.

And Hazell? He wheeled away to take 14 wickets for 139. That left Gimblett only time to bowl two overs of his amiable seamers. We shall never know how he managed to squeeze in 30 overs between his prodigious hitting at Manchester.

Gimblett relished the Northamptonshire bowling at Kettering. Dear, lowly Northants had, like Somerset, often had to live with ignominy and the cheap jibes of unfeeling pundits. They came back to Bath in June and the Bicknoller Blaster scored 143 in the second innings. It was his fourth century of the season and he completed his 1,000 runs. The second 50 came in 37 minutes.

Bath was good for my expenses – I stayed with Rita's aunt. It was, over the years, also good for my averages. I remember in the Northants match I went from 70 to 142 in boundaries. At one point, Nobby Clark said impatiently, 'Give me the ball.' Arthur Bakewell, who was at square leg, muttered to me: 'Well, Harold, you can go and take a walk round the Abbey for a couple of hours. When Nobby calls for the ball like that, he's going to let fly a few bouncers. You won't get near 'em.' Nobby started firing the ball short – and I began whacking them.

At the other end J. E. Buswell, a well-built fellow with wavy hair, good club standard as a fast bowler, hurled a few hopefully down. I put one on the roof of the pavilion with a straight drive.

After the match he came up and thanked me. I just couldn't understand why. 'I'm dead serious. Well, I thought I was good enough for county cricket. But you taught me something I knew nothing about. When you hit me back over my head, first class cricket and myself went in different directions.' He was a nice chap. And he did get Reggie Ingle, his only wicket.

Gimblett discovered that opposing pros were not jealous of his successes, though they may have doubted his ability to keep it up at his ferocious, carefree pace. At the Oval, he was warmly wished good luck by Alf Gover, Ted Brooks, Stan Squires, Bob Gregory and Eddie Watts. Harold settled for a modest 50. At the end of one over, he idly picked up the ball. It looked remarkably new and polished, considering the match had been going for three-quarters of an hour.

I smelt it. It was the most beautifully smelling ball I'd ever come across. I turned to the umpire and joked innocently that someone had got some nice haircream. He called over the skipper, E. R. T. Holmes. 'One of your lads has got too much hair oil on his cap!' And then, with a change of tone: 'Tell him to cut it out.' Of course, it was Alf Gover. I was wide-eyed . . . the country boy. For the next two overs I was given the roughest treatment I'd ever known. Alf fired his cannon balls at me. He only hit me once – and that was enough.

Before that game against Surrey, a slim, dark-suited man came into the Somerset dressing room. He had given up cricket by then; he carried an umbrella and not a bat. He shook Gimblett's hand. 'I've heard all about you and I've come to wish you all the best.'

It was Jack Hobbs. He'd bothered to make a special journey to do this. It was one of the supreme moments in my life. Sadly I only saw him play once, ten years earlier when he scored his 126th century, at Taunton, to equal W. G. Grace's record. He kept everyone waiting till the Monday morning and then kept us in agony while he was caught off a no-ball. In the next innings, he beat W.G.'s record. He's the only cricketer I can think of about whom no one ever made a derogatory remark. He must have been a wonderful man.

In late June, to the immeasurable delight of all whose pulses quickened at the sight of a batsman who dared, Gimblett was chosen to make his Test debut against the Indians at Lord's. Everyone had been telling the selectors for weeks that they should go hotfoot to Taunton. They happily decided on Kettering where unconsciously he obliged them with a century before lunch.

Honestly I didn't know enough about cricket to play for my country. I wasn't even a quarter ready for it . . . I can remember listening to the twelve names announced on the radio. The names were given in alphabetical order and I prayed that I wouldn't be included. Far from throwing my hat in the air, I was terrified. Suddenly I realized the fearful responsibilities resting on my shoulders. The telephone started ringing, cars arrived, the usual nonsense.

I just wanted to go away and get lost. I didn't want to play for England. In desperation I jumped on my bicycle and went in search of Rita.

Gubby Allen captained England and put the Indians in. England won by nine wickets and Gimblett's second innings knock of 67 not out was the highest individual one of the game. He had earlier gone for 11. It was never certain how easy the ultimate winning total of 107 would be in this miserably low-scoring match. The debutant started with a few of his beloved, if fallible, hooks; later when Nissar was brought back, Gimblett stroked four successive balls to the boundary – and it was virtually over.

The Times thundered sensationally: 'This was a glorious innings by Gimblett. He is a splendid opening batsman who on any kind of wicket is a run maker. If there is anyone except Duckworth and Leyland who must always play for England, it is Gimblett.'

With greater reservation, E. W. Swanton was to write in *A History of Cricket* like this: 'Gimblett was chosen for England in his second season, and at that time many extravagant things were prophesied for him. From one cause or another, the highest hopes were not fulfilled. The advent concurrently of Hutton and Compton decreased the number of Test batting places. Perhaps, too, Gimblett may have suffered from the traditional conservatism of English selectors who when it comes to the point, tend to prefer safety to brilliance. I am not quite sure that Gimblett was fired with the intensity of ambition that generally characterizes those who shoulder their way to the top of the tree. At all events, whether or not Gimblett was a loss to England, his attractive, wristy play for his county gave more pleasure to a larger number than many who achieved greater fame.'

Yet who would dare call the first Test a failure for the Somerset player? It had been a plentiful and juicy year in the Somerset orchards, and now cider flowed at Bicknoller. Watchet and 'W.G.' said we told you so; so did Jack Hurley the scribe from Williton, and the masters at West Buckland.

Gimblett received £17-10s for playing at Lord's. The team stayed at the Great Eastern, the first time Harold had ever slept in a big hotel. 'It was a bit different from the cramped digs at Paddington and Bayswater,' he said later.

In the course of our chats, Gimblett told me many absorbing stories: none more so than what happened off the field during that Lord's Test match.

It was only my second visit to the ground. I arrived by 10.30 a.m. and walked shyly through the Long Room to the dressing rooms. Then I heard this hum, this buzz outside and I looked through the window. There were 30,000 people out there waiting to see us play. Oh dear! Then I was rescued from my panic. Hedley Verity and Maurice Leyland said: 'Come on over here and sit with us. We'll look after you.' I really believe that if they hadn't done that, I'd have followed my instincts and raced away from the ground.

I was so grateful that we didn't bat first. But when it was my turn I was all at sea against the inswing of Amar Singh and was out. I was so miserable and upset. I didn't want anyone to recognize me, so I put on my civvy clothes and started wandering round the ground. I was disconsolate and there was this horrible black cloud. Here I was playing for England and I'd made a hash of it.

Suddenly I heard this voice. 'Whoever's trodden on your foot, Harold?' It was Jack Hobbs, in the crowd, near the clock. 'Oh, Jack, did you see my performance?' He said I'd made eleven and that was better than some of them. And he went on: 'You had your feet in the wrong place, that's all. Here, come and have a cup of tea.'

Scores of people recognized him. No one knew who I was. He chatted encouragingly to me over our cuppa. Then with his umbrella he explained the technique of playing inswing bowling.

I'm convinced that even at his age he could have gone out with his umbrella and still made runs for England.

Jack's kindly advice made all the difference in the second innings. I got my feet into the right place for inswing. Arthur Mitchell had a brute of a first ball and was out in the gully. In came Maurice Turnbull and I now had the confidence to look after Amar Singh. When we returned to the Long Room, the members made a line for us. Even the fossils who'd sat on their stools impassively for the three days got to their feet and applauded. Everyone said to me: 'Well done.'

Whatever the earlier spells of mental trauma, there was blissfully also the humour. During the match, a number of the players decided to have a rather special evening meal in the West End. Young Harold was mesmerized by the etiquette among the waiters. The head waiter fussed and affected to know most of the team. He discreetly ignored the slightly awkward West Country lad in his sports jacket. Steaks were ordered and duly arrived. All the party except Gimblett grasped knives and forks; he remained, inactive, looking disbelievingly at his meat.

The head waiter, with a patronizing curl of the lips, sidled over. 'Is everything to your liking, em – sir?'

The affable Leyland and the others were by now watching, not sure what was going to happen.

Harold met the head waiter's smirky gaze. 'Is there anything wrong?'

'This sirloin steak,' said Gimblett, very deliberately. 'Now I know I'm only twenty-one and not very worldly. But for three generations we've reared these animals. And yet is this all we're getting from a superb Devon steer? Something must be wrong somewhere.'

The farmer's son momentarily had the floor to himself. Bill Bowes and his teammates didn't know what to say. They were hungry and had not intended complaining.

In a flash, the head waiter nodded to his staff. All the plates were swept from the table in a single movement and returned to the kitchen. Leyland blurted: 'Ee, lad, what's thou doon? They've left us with noothin' to eat.'

There was a delayed, rather embarrassed silence. Within ten minutes, back came the retinue of waiters, bearing enormous, lusciously grilled steaks. They were tender and beautifully garnished. The England players had no room left for their sweets.

Leyland winked and said: 'We must bring the boy again.'

All that and a Novello musical to follow. And gentle, helpful words from Jack Hobbs. Maybe cricket was not so bad after all.

Gimblett kept his place for the second Test, at Old Trafford towards the end of July. It gave him no pleasure at all. He hit two searing fours through the covers in no time at all and was out for 9. England went on to make 571. Arthur Fagg made his Test debut and opened with Gimblett. Nearly everyone made runs. Hammond scored 167 and Hardstaff 94. Worthington helped himself to 87; R. W. V. Robins, at No. 8, made 76. Verity, at No. 9, was 66 not out. The Somerset boy dropped a sitter 'and got headlines for it'.

Rain came on the third day and he did not have another chance to bat in a drawn match. He was dropped for the next Test. 'Thank goodness that's over!' he said to anyone within earshot.

In a season which had started marvellously and brought him almost unheard-of Test recognition, he dived into introspection and self-criticism. Why did Reg Perks and Laurie Gray get him out so easily? When it came to the final fixture, against Lancashire at Taunton, there was a sudden outpouring of despair to Eddie Phillipson.

'Eddie, I can't get a run for love or money. I'm thinking of chucking the whole thing.'

Phillipson was in a benevolent mood at this stage of the season. 'O.K., Harold, I'll give you a few and get you started again.'

For two overs he sent down half-volleys outside the off stump. 'Thanks, Eddie.'

'Want any more?' Gimblett grinned and shook his head. Those fours, cracked through the covers, were more timely than many of his 49 centuries for the county.

In any context, 1936 was an eventful season for him. He ended with an average of 32.81 and that should have pleased him, so early in his career. Instead the acclaim dissolved to self-imposed solitude. The Lord's and Old Trafford Tests became painful rather than treasured memories; he pleaded silently that he would not ever be selected again. It was a rejection of honour that ironically conflicted with the fervent hopes of thousands of cricket lovers, not all of them from his native West Country.

One of the positive features of the summer was that he had been turned into an opening batsman. He put it down to circumstances – the departure of Jack Lee – rather than an inspired hunch from anyone on the committee.

Jack, who opened with brother Frank, was due a benefit though no one said anything officially. He went in to see the secretary and said that Mill House School were offering him more than £300 a year if he went coaching there. We shall never know how much the popular Lee was gambling. Somerset were not particularly gracious when it came to rewarding loyalty. The abrupt answer given to Jack was: 'Take it.' It was a pragmatic response that shocked some of Lee's teammates including Gimblett. 'That,' he said, 'typified the county's attitude. They hadn't the slightest idea what a fine cricketer he was. If one of their serfs wanted to leave, who cared?'

I have written of Gimblett's beneficial liaison with Jack Hobbs in 1936. There were also discussions with Herbert Sutcliffe and Wally Hammond.

I gradually came to like John Daniell. Behind the façade was a good man. But he could be a terror to anyone new on the staff. He knew I loved hooking and I was getting caught in all sorts of places. There was the time he came to me and said: 'The committee have instructed me to inform you to stop hooking.' Think of that – ugh! You can imagine how I reacted.

But I was honest enough to know I was having problems with the shot. When we got to Sheffield in the August of 1936 it was raining, I remember, and I was walking round the pavilion. I saw Herbert Sutcliffe sitting in a corner on his own. I was a bit diffident about approaching him. 'Em – can you help me, Mr Sutcliffe?'

'Come and sit down, son. Let's hear about it.'

I told him of Somerset's pompous instructions – I had to cut out the hook.

'Do you like hooking?'

'Well, in club cricket, if someone dropped a ball short it was always four free runs.'

Herbert looked at me approvingly. 'That's the right attitude, son. So all we have to do is get you in the correct position for it. Now listen, when the bowler gets to within five or six yards of the wicket, slide your right foot straight across the crease to the off stump. You're not off balance – you can go back or forwards. All you have to do then is whack it for four.'

That was the day, a rainy one at Sheffield, when I learned to hook. And I like to think that by the end I was one of the best around.

84

...akes Farm, where Harold
...s born.

...George's Church, Bick-
...ller, aloft of which is the
...eather-cock which still bears
...e signs of a youthful Gim-
...ett prank.

Two Watchet lads together.
Harold (*left*) and Alan Pearse,
who played in the same Sòm-
erset side against Kent at
Frome in 1936.

Harold and Rita on their wedding day. But positively no
press photographs . . .

A 1938 Somerset team. *Back row l to r:* Hazell, Buse, Wellard, Reg Trump (scorer), Andrews, Lee, Gimblett. *Front row l to r:* Luckes, M. D. Lyon, Longrigg, J. W. Seamer, K. C. Kinnersley.

Only his second m
for Somerset. He
Robins to leg at L
Middlesex win by s
wickets but Gimbl
his county's top s
(53).

Six of the Somerset pros in 1938. *L to r*: Wally Luckes, Harold Gimblett, Frank Lee, Bill Andrews, Arthur Wellard and Bertie Buse.

The 1946 team.

SOMERSET C.C.C. 1946

SOMERSET C.C.C.

BACK ROW (L.to R.):—
H. GIMBLETT,
F.S. LEE,
A. WELLARD,
R. TRUMP (Scorer),
W. ANDREWS,
H. BUSE,
J. LAWRENCE.
FRONT ROW (L.to R.):—
W. LUCKES,
A.T. JONES,
N.S. MITCHELL-INNES,
E.F. LONGRIGG (Capt.),
C.J.P. BARNWELL,
G.R. LANGDALE.

F.S. LEE
BENEFIT SEASON 1947.

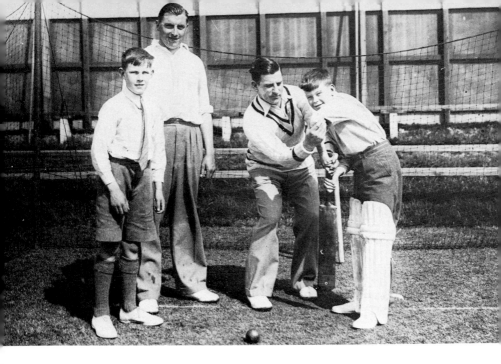

Harold and Wally Luckes helping boys with the coaching at the Taunton nets before the war.

A fine opening partnership. Frank Lee and Harold, friends off the field, go out to bat in a prewar match.

The early Fifties: a combined Somerset and trialists' group. *Back, l to r*: M. Walker, E. Robinson, H. Hazell, H. Stephenson, L. Angell. *Middle row*: A. Thomas, C. Davey, B. Buse, H. Gimblett, M. Tremlett, E. Wormersley, W. Deane. *Front row*: J. Redman, H. Parks (coach), S. Rogers, J. Lawrence, R. Smith, S. Cray, D. Kitson.

Harold strokes a typical cover boundary, this time at the county ground in Bristol, 1953. Andy Wilson is the wicket keeper.

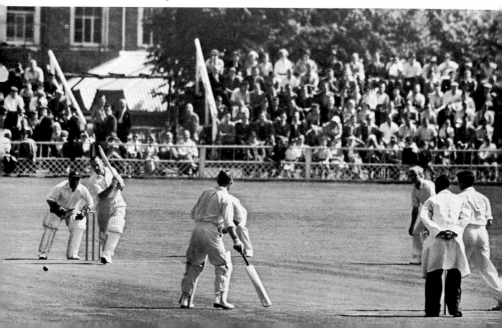

On the way to his benefit hundred against Northants at Glastonbury in 1952. The late Ron Roberts, then a West Country journalist and confidant of Gimblett, can be seen in the small press tent.

Harold's last appearance. He takes part in a special centenary match against a celebrity side at Clarence Park, Weston-super-Mare in 1975. *Seated*: H. D. Burrough, C. J. P. Barnwell, A. Wellard, B. Hockin, W. Andrews, H. Stephenson, H. Gimblett, M. Tremlett. *Standing*: D. Foot (author), B. Lobb (behind), F. Lee, Alec Stock, D. Robinson, M. Kitchen, D. Waine, Ted Drake, D. Allen, J. Parks, A. T. M. Jones, P. Davies, A. C. H. Smith, P. Wight, L. Clark, L. Angell, Trevor Bannister, J. Lawrence, D. Solomons, G. Petherbridge.

Harold in contemplative mood, recovering from an early operation.

A few days before his death at Verwood. Harold leans on a stick, supported by his wife (*left*) and a visiting friend.

Someone, maybe one of the canny well-wishers at Watchet, had clearly advised Gimblett: 'If you want to be put right on anything, go to a Master.' It proved an invaluable word in the ear. School coaching was negligible: those in charge, to their eternal credit, left him to pursue his forceful cricket in his own uncomplicated way. As a county cricketer – and one with an inferiority complex – he acknowledged the deficiencies in his technical approach. Now we come to Hammond.

Gimblett had been schooled in the winsome ways of village cricket. But on his own initiative, no easy matter for an introvert, he had learned from great players how to cope with inswing and how to play the hook. It was now time, he decided, to come to terms with leg break and the googlie.

I'd been getting myself out a few times to them in the oddest manner. Essex's Peter Smith gave me my first experience of the breed. But, in fact, he never seemed to me a genuine leg spinner. He was a bit of a roller. He didn't give it a real flip like some of them did.

When we were playing Gloucestershire I approached Walter Hammond. Just like Herbert Sutcliffe had done, Wally sensed I was troubled.

'It's these leg breaks and googlies,' I said.

'What are they?' he replied, with as much of a twinkle as he was ever likely to reveal.

'You know,' I said, embarrassed, 'the googlie's the one you think is going one way and it goes in the opposite.'

Hammond gave me a long stare. 'Forget 'em, Harold. Ignore 'em.'

'That's all very well for you,' I said. 'You can play them with your eyes shut. It's something I haven't learned to do.'

'First of all, clear your mind of this nonsense about them turning one way or the other. Just play every ball *on its merit where it pitches.*'

Hammond was not an easy man to talk to. But he was very helpful to me. He explained that if the ball was a half-volley

85

I should aim for somewhere between mid on and mid off, that arc. If it was a leg spinner, the shot would go past mid off, hopefully for four. Or for the googlie, it would go past mid on.

'There's one golden rule,' he said. 'Normally to play back, you're supposed to get into a position where you are absolutely right behind the ball. But not with these boys. They can catch you with a top spinner or one that hurries off the wicket. You've got to give yourself a bit of room. Go forwards and backwards on the leg stump. If it's slightly short, you can play back and, outside the off stump, you have all the arc in the world, square to cover point and beyond, to hit it where you like as hard as you like. If it comes into you (googlie) you've still got plenty of time and room to play wide of mid on for 2, 3 or 4.'

I couldn't wait for leg spinners after that. Yes, all right, Doug Wright did get me out three times in four balls from him. By the time I worked out what to do, Doug – at medium pace – had beaten me. But he never got me again and, my goodness, I took him apart a few times. At Gravesend, he looked down the wicket at me and said: 'I just don't know where to bowl the next one, Harold.'

My reluctance to move on from 1936 is, I hope, understandable. It contained so many peaks and so much human drama. The engrossing paradoxes tumbled over each other. I leave the season with one final story. He told me about it but could not remember the match.

In the last over of the day someone bowled him a full toss. It may have reflected fatigue or cunning. Gimblett always treated such luxuries in the same dismissive manner. He heaved the ball on to the tea stall at Taunton. 'That was me. I had no regrets.'

It was a sentiment not shared by his captain. 'If you ever play a shot like that again in the final over you'll be dropped.' The young batsman was stunned. He had been through a lean, depressing spell and now, after some sturdy blows to the boundary, he felt he deserved a warmer greeting.

Gimblett strode into the dressing room and slumped on a bench. 'Who's in next?' he asked angrily to no one in particular. 'Get your pads on early in the morning. I won't be hanging around when I get to the wicket.' Nor was he. The young batsman, still smarting from his captain's rebuke, was out in the first over.

There was more trouble for him on the third day. Somerset needed to make a hasty exit at the close of play, to catch a 6.30 p.m. train for the away fixture that followed. He was one of the last to leave the field and then, reminded of the acute need for speed, knotted a tie on his cricket shirt and pulled on his other trousers.

On the station platform he was publicly criticized for supposedly having on a dirty shirt.

He was invariably well groomed and a neat, if unostentatious, dresser. The reprimand rankled.

Inspiration for a sermon

There were 1,558 runs and three centuries in 1937. Who was complaining? Some of the purists were, more and more. They winced as he flexed his muscles at the new-ball bowlers. They rumbled in agitation as the occasional hook, over ambitious and still not sufficiently disciplined by Sutcliffe's words, ended in a pathetic little catch close in on the leg side. 'Is he never going to learn?' they asked, forgetting his mighty and majestic innings.

At times he was dropped to No. 4. Bertie Buse opened with Frank Lee; so did Sydney Rippon and Jack Meyer. When Lee was hurt during the game at Trent Bridge, Gimblett moved back to the top of the order and made his cussed point with a 94. At Newport he took just over two hours to score an undefeated 129; at Bristol, he reached a century in 95 minutes. Wells is renowned for its cathedral and its clergy who patrol the somnolent streets in pairs like preoccupied umpires on the way to the wicket. Wellard twiced rocked the cloistered calm there with five blasphemous sixes in an over. In 1937 against Hampshire, it was Gimblett's turn. He scored a fiery and faultless 141: they came in a blaze of scoring shots, including nine sixes and sixteen fours. And they inspired many a sermon.

'I just hate being tied down. Once I lose my adventurous style I may as well pack the whole thing in,' he told friends when they complimented him on his aggression and daring.

It was always possible to equate that aggression with natural panache. His cover and straight drive were superb. His hook was, well, daring. He had a sense of theatre and would suddenly stage-manage an unorthodox shot of gargantuan proportions. It was usually predetermined in its utter safety.

'Once at Taunton I got too cocky and played a dreadful shot. It got me out and I was very angry with myself.' As he came in, a member shouted: 'What a bloody awful shot, Gimblett.' The batsman stopped in his tracks and gripped the handle of his bat belligerently. 'How I didn't crown him, I'll never know.'

By now the young bachelor had saved a little money. He bought his first car, a Singer Bantam. In the winter months he took up shooting and hunting. He had always been a menace to the local rabbit population. With three friends he formed a rabbit-catching syndicate. They each put £5 into the kitty and for five days a week went after their furry prey. 'It was quite profitable and we acquired something of a reputation around the Quantocks. One day we put four ferrets in, and two dogs as well. Then we stationed ourselves and waited. Out the rabbits came. In three hours I had 49 shots and killed 48 rabbits.'

He had an ambivalent approach to stag hunting. He could remember, as a boy, how the stags came at night to eat the swedes, turnips and corn on the farm; he accepted that there was a need for some control. He also knew all about the poachers and the excellent prices offered for carcasses. The thought of a wounded deer, its body full of buckshot, filled him with repugnance. Once in the old deer park at St Audries, he caught a deer in flight. It had been chased and hadn't enough wind left to jump the railings. In panic, it came straight at Harold and he brought it down with a rugby tackle. A huntsman arrived with a humane killer.

'I don't know what possessed me – I did it without thinking. I was given the hoof and had it mounted in a cabinet at home. But the whole business filled me with self-doubts. The stag was a magnificent animal, too beautiful to chase or shoot. Every time I saw one, a shiver went up my spine. In later years, of course, I couldn't have shot a cock pheasant if someone had handed me a gun and then thrown the pheasant up in the air in front of me.'

Gimblett turned up in his little Singer for the start of the 1938 season. His career did not noticeably progress, though Somerset were in no position to sniff at 1,304 runs. The batting average dipped under 30 for the first time in three years, and seven wickets in 46 overs hardly ranked as compensation.

He was never completely fit even if he still played in 29 matches. Back in the dressing room he complained of aches and pains. At the crease he was more circumspect. He grafted, more strikingly than ever before, for 91 in the opening match at Hove; that set a new pattern. There was restraint and a new-found discrimination during his century at Folkestone. As if to remind his audience that it was not his true nature, he paraded a succession of wonderful drives to reach his second 50 in 35 minutes.

Varying counsel was being offered him. He seemed to be taking some notice of those who wanted him to tighten his defence. A tardy scoreboard was never to his liking. His impatience showed and he was out. He relished his reputation as a hitter and it did not suit his pride to become a plodder. Not that he was ever that. Half-volleys were still unfailingly despatched. Sixes were statistically in the Wellard class, even if they did not reach the same altitude.

Essex had long memories. They never quite forgave him for the savagery of his upstart shots against them on his debut. This time they twice got him for a duck at Bath. He went off to Kettering and hit another century at the expense of Northamptonshire. It was probably his worst; Timms deserved to get him three times in one embarrassing over. He flopped against the Australians when they arrived at Taunton. Dar Lyon opened with Lee; Gimblett was relegated to No. 5 and made 7 and 6. He played through the match with an air almost of indifference. Are we to read anything into his failure against the Tourists? Yes, in view of what he emphatically said later about playing for his country, I think we are.

There was at least a wedding to look forward to. It took place in the December at Watchet. Almost every pew was filled; outside there was snow on the ground. After the service, Harold had to pay a traditional toll as part of a local custom. The bride and groom were chained and only released when the silver was handed over. He upset some of the local photographers who had waited patiently in the cold. They were waved away. There were no official press wedding photos.

Harold and Rita moved into their first house, at Taunton. He argued that it was preferable to a 20-mile journey to Bicknoller on a night when the team arrived back in Somerset at half past two in the morning. The couple furnished their house for £127. From a winter job, he learned the basics of carpentry and other practical jobs about the house. In the whole of his married life he seldom used outside labour for maintenance.

Gimblett scored just under 2,000 runs in 1939 and was recalled for a Test match against the West Indies. There were 905 runs in his first seven matches; five centuries came in consecutive fixtures. Married life was suiting him.

He and Lee built up a reputation for their three-figure opening stands. Their methods were different; their rapport when it came to running between the wickets was almost flawless. They were friends off the field: among the quiet conversationists rather than the more boisterous drinkers in the team. They never feared the new ball and opponents tried in vain for an early breakthrough.

The England selectors watched or, more often, noted Gimblett's stylish, punchy hundreds against Lancashire, Sussex, Leicestershire, Gloucestershire and Worcestershire. Those centuries just came, one after the other with only token breaks. Three were at Taunton, to the immense vocal delight of Somerset supporters. A Saturday century by Gimblett was the surest bet in the West. With a risible aberration, he was out for a duck in the match with Oxford University at Bath. The selectors wisely took

90

no notice of his lapse against the undergraduates. He was chosen to play for England at Lord's in late June. His opening partner was Len Hutton.

J. H. Cameron, the son of a West Indian doctor, bowled him for 22 in the first innings. The little googlie bowler's success had an ironic twist. He was educated at Taunton School, where his extravagant and inaccurate spinners were apt to disconcert most of the opposition. In a public schools' trial at Lord's he once took all ten wickets in an innings. Somerset decided he was too promising to let go. His bowling for the county was altogether less memorable; but he at least once topped the batting averages, and also scored runs rather than took wickets when he went up to Cambridge. Now, in 1939, he was back as vice captain of the touring side.

Little Cameron came on at the pavilion end and chucked one up into the air. I lost it completely. I played back when I should have gone forward. He bowled me all over the place. Perhaps it was a good thing I was out . . . yes, I think it was. I'd actually blotted my copy book by hitting Les Hylton into the stand with the first ball I received. You don't do that in a Test – and at Lord's. After I'd gone, Len Hutton and Denis Compton produced some champagne cricket between lunch and tea. Len was at his supreme best in getting 196 but Denis sometimes surpassed him. I could only look on in admiration.

We only needed 99 for victory at the end. I hooked Hylton's first two deliveries for four and six, and was out for 20, bowled by Martindale as I tried to get things over quickly. That was the end of my Test career.

Some things I remember – like the catch I took. Bill Copson was bowling from the nursery end and I was the only man on the offside in front of the wicket. Weekes, the left-hander, slashed at one. It soared away to my left at cover point.

It was too square for third man so instinctively I decided I'd better go for it. I went like a hare. It seemed an awful long way and nothing appeared to be happening as I lost the ball. Then it suddenly dropped over my right shoulder, as I ran. It pounded into my right hand and stuck. I didn't really see it from the moment it left the bat. I later heard a repeat of Howard Marshall's broadcast and he said it was the greatest catch he'd ever seen. Not only the finest – but the biggest fluke, I'm telling you!

The next man in was Learie Constantine. He did a little diversion to speak to me. He patted me on the back and said 'Well done.' It was a lovely bonus.

I must tell you of the next time we played in the same match. It was the Victory Test and Learie was captaining the World XI. We hadn't met before the match. Then he came on to bowl and he was still pretty fast. He hit me three times in four balls on the inside of the right leg. It's a golden rule for a batsman not to flinch when he's hit on the leg. I did my best not to. The first time he got me, I grimaced with pain and did nothing. The second time, I found myself rubbing the leg. And when he hit me a third time, the bat flew out of my hand one way and the gloves came off in another. Tears welled up in my eyes. I saw Learie coming down the wicket in sympathy. I just had, in my pain, to say something. And I blurted out: 'Oh, you . . . you black man!' He took it well and laughed. Just laughed.

We met once more, in the Sixties. I was asked to umpire a Rothmans match which was televised. By then, Learie was knighted, very much an establishment figure. The game was at Taunton and I arrived from the car park. Then I spotted him, ten yards or so away. He hadn't seen me. I approached him from behind and quietly said 'Black man!' He didn't turn. Then he said: 'There's only one man in the world could say that to me.' He put both hands on my shoulders, in greeting.

But I began by talking of playing against him in the 1939 Lord's Test. I was only in for the one. Wally Hammond, I remember, tried to frighten me by making me field two yards from the bat. Howard Marshall said that if George Headley wasn't looking, I could put out my hand and pick his pockets. I had complete confidence in the fast bowlers. George got a century in both innings – but he shouldn't have. I'm pretty sure I ran him out in the first innings, with a throw which hit the wickets from the boundary. And then I should probably have caught him in the second. I was half an inch out with my final dive. It cost me 1/6 to get my trousers cleaned. But Headley was magnificent.

That was it. At the age of 24, it was goodbye to England. The war saw to that, in any case. Gimblett's brief Test career, spread over three years, was in no sense a disaster. There were comparisons with Frank Woolley and others who dared. He hooked out of sheer devilment, just as Ian Botham was to do more than forty years later. He played shots that, at Test time, Lord's was not used to. The selectors saw the virtues of his batting – and the risk they themselves took.

There was one other honour for him before the war. He found himself opening the batting again with Hutton, this time for the Players against the Gentlemen. It was a way for him to exorcize the class system iniquities, as he saw them. 'We're still the lowest form of animal life,' he told his teammates. There was venom, far beyond the cricket field, in the exceptional aggression of his stroke-making, as he scored a brilliant half-century in the first innings.

In fact, social patterns were already changing. The war would complete the metamorphosis. But Gimblett sensed no new breeze of democracy as he flung his bat, with figurative fury, at the Gentlemen.

R. W. V. Robins was one of those pre-war amateurs none too lovingly regarded by Gimblett. He could be tetchy as I discovered from my own practical journalistic experience. The Somerset man's disaffection may even have emanated from the fact that Robins dismissed him the first time he batted at Lord's, in 1935 immediately after the Frome debut.

In the late August of 1939, Somerset were at Lord's and Gimblett was enjoying himself at the expense of Sims, Gray and Smith. Then he heard a liverish Robins say: 'I'll have the next one. I can get this blighter out any day.'

It was a stage whisper and the batsman bristled. He carefully played three overs and then went after Robins. One straight drive was 'as ferocious as I could make it'. The bowler threw his hands up to protect his face. He badly split his right hand and had to retire.

'Blimey, it almost looked deliberate, Gimbo,' one of the Somerset players said. There was no audible answer.

It was hardly a vendetta but it almost appeared like one. The Somerset dressing room was a good-humoured, even light-hearted, community. Players, including Harold, joked about 'The Stogumber', the unorthodox shot made famous by the West Somerset parish's most famous resident, J. C. White. There were various versions: the most accurate was the affected straight drive that miraculously turned into a sweep to square leg. Wellard, Andrews and Hazell were a reliable trinity to lift spirits when they were down. Hazell was known to put a towel round his head, strip to the waist and offer a prayer for rain to Allah. He did it once at Clacton, when Somerset were hopelessly placed and there were azure skies everywhere. Within half an hour the ground was flooded.

'One of the miracles of Somerset cricket,' Gimblett always said.

The war came – and it was time for reckoning in every sense. In just four and a half seasons, he had scored very nearly 7,000 runs. He had picked up a few well spaced wickets and held 78 catches. Once or twice he had done badly in the slips in front of people who mattered; but his outfielding had given Somerset a verve it had seldom possessed before. 'Harold could throw straight into the stumper's gloves every time. That was an untold luxury for us. In the days of dear old C. C. C. Case, the ball bounced three times before it got back to the wicket,' an ex-player confided.

The first time Gimblett played on the county ground was as a schoolboy for West Buckland. His English master Sammy Howells was thrilled to see the boy take 7–49 in an unimportant fixture long since forgotten. At the end of his spell, a bouncy giant of a man slapped him on the back. 'Off spinners, weren't they, son? Just stick to them and you'll play for Somerset one day.'

94

Young Gimblett treated the prophecy as a joke, even though the giant's name was Sammy Woods. Everyone – on a skittle alley or a harvest home, as well as a cricket ground – knew Sammy. His generous words to Harold were the subject of much envy over tea.

Gimblett had no wish to play for Somerset and, in any case, he did not stick to off spinners.

S. M. J. Woods, who played cricket for Australia and England, rugby for England, and sang for anyone who offered him a drink and an evening's friendship, had impeccable sporting judgement. But he was at least partly wrong about Gimblett.

There were no off breaks to make the headlines at Frome in 1935.

Then the war

Harold and Rita had planned a short holiday in Scotland and set off on the journey with an intended stop at Scarborough on the way. They never reached Scotland: Hitler saw to that. War was declared and they returned to Taunton immediately.

Gimblett ended up in the Fire Service and not the Armed Forces. Some of his cricketing contemporaries argue that he was consumed with guilt about this. His own words are revealing and fit into the overall pattern of his troubled and complicated life.

I suppose I should have gone and volunteered. It was one of those things that left a scar on my mind.

At the same time, let us authenticate what actually happened. His inclination was to join the Royal Air Force and he was summoned to Exeter, along with 32 others on a Saturday morning, for his interview. The ritual always had a wry humour about it. In Gimblett's case, he recognized the recruiting officer who, in his important role and freshly creased new uniform, pretended not to know him.

95

'Let's see . . . Gimblett H. . . . so you want to go in the R.A.F. Fighter pilot?'

'I can't stand speed – too fast for me,' replied Gimblett.

'Bomber pilot?'

'Can't see at night.'

'Ah, well then, rear gunner . . .'

'I can't travel with my back to the engine.'

Slightly exasperated, the recruiting officer said the best thing for Gimblett would be for him to report to Blackpool, where they would sort him out somehow or other.

For the record, he was one of the few among the 33 at Exeter that morning who passed A1. When it had come to the medical, he had gone behind a screen with eight others to provide a urine sample. 'All the others were having acute trouble. I gave the eight of them a sample. It may sound slightly crude but it happened.'

A fortnight after his interview he received a familiar buff envelope through the post. It contained the surprising news that he was to report to the fire station at Taunton. 'So I became a fireman. Many times I thought it was not quite right. I'd have sooner gone into the Air Force.'

In truth, his wartime experiences showed him to be an efficient fireman – and a brave one. He was in the middle of many serious blitzes. 'At Plymouth, Bristol, Avonmouth, Bath and Exeter, I saw the terrible side of war and I saw heroism of the kind I never thought possible.' There were 550 firemen rushed into service for one horrific raid on Plymouth. 'I saw so many sides of human nature. In Plymouth I was sent to help save a church. When we got there, we discovered a basket of incendiaries going well, up in the roof. Our ladders weren't high enough and we tried to knock the incendiaries off with our jets. There was water everywhere. The vicar gave us a pasting and actually swore at me for desecrating his church. Next night a high explosive went through the roof.'

He was much moved and permanently affected when members of his crew were killed. 'There was a raid on Bristol on a Good Friday night and there was a direct hit on the building. Four of my chaps were killed outright. Another had his leg blown off. I was stunned. I couldn't think. I didn't know what to do.'

A few days later he visited the casualty in hospital at Taunton. 'I crept up to Arthur Fletcher's bed and gently touched him. He opened his blue eyes and told me he was going to have a wooden leg, so would be able to make a fortune planting potatoes!'

Ronald Priddle, who ended up as Harold's station commander, and briefly slept in the same dormitory, confirmed how upset Gimblett was over the deaths of his colleagues. He was often depressed by the scenes of destruction he had experienced. As a section leader he had twenty men under him. 'They thought the world of him.'

There is some evidence that he preferred not to have responsibility when tackling a fire. He would willingly pass decision-making to a senior officer if there was one in the vicinity. His dormitory locker was full of pills.

He was not always morose, it seems, during off-duty hours. The firemen, their eyes heavy from continuous lack of sleep, still looked for light-hearted diversion. They basked in Gimblett's sporting fame and looked to him for cricketing anecdotes. County cricket was already a distant dream but the sharpness of his eye had not lessened from the smarting smoke of city ruins.

The much requested party piece in the firemen's dormitory involved an act of astonishing skill, if not vandalism. He would invite his colleagues to nominate one of the electric light bulbs. Someone would pass him a broom handle and then throw a tennis ball. With hook or even straight drive he would smash the bulb with uncanny regularity.

A number of one-day matches were arranged for Lord's. Gimblett was chosen for the Civil Defence, to play against the Army or Air Force. The games attracted huge crowds; there was an indescribable joy and sense of escape about the occasion. Battle-weary cricket lovers came together to pretend just for a day that things were normal. Maybe it was something of a charade but it transcended the horrors of war. Proceeds went to the Red Cross.

In the June of 1943, Gimblett was invited to play against the Army. He had at that point hardly picked up a bat for more than two years. Sir Pelham Warner wrote glowingly of the match, which the Civil Defence won by six wickets. The illustrious author, whatever his minor contretemps with the young Somerset batsman in the Thirties, extolled the way Gimblett scored 124 in 100 minutes. 'He made one remarkable stroke. The wicket was pitched rather away from the middle, some 15 yards up towards the Grand Stand, and he hooked a ball from Nichols, the Essex bowler, full pitch into the middle of the Mound Stand. Some newspapers asserted it carried 150 yards. It was scarcely that but certainly near 130 yards, and although longer drives have been made at Lord's, this must be a record hook stroke . . . It was a great match, and 505 runs were scored.'

All that time without touching a bat – and here I was middling it from the first ball. Don't ask me how. We turned up with four opening bats, I remember – John Langridge, Jim Parks, Johnny Arnold and myself. So we drew lots and I went in No. 4. From an entertainment point of view, it was one of the best knocks I ever played. Stan Nichols was a rattling good bowler but I managed to hit him straight back for four. I think he took umbrage a bit. He let go this bouncer at me. And it was last seen halfway up the Mound Stand. I heard later that a man stuck out his hand to protect a woman spectator and he broke his fingers. A cricket writer paced out the shot and it was thought to be the longest hook on record in this country.

Gimblett loved the hook. He was less loving towards those who attempted to dissuade him from using it.

Soon after the war the M.C.C. encouraged Harry Crabtree, of Essex, to produce an official coaching manual. It found no favour at all with Gimblett.

How could you play cricket by numbers, I asked myself? I've seen all the great players of my age. But I've never seen two players do things in exactly the same way. How can you line up ten boys against a wall and tell them they must play a particular shot in an absolutely identical way. I'm all for Sinatra doing it his way. The youngster must do what is *natural* for him. The business of the coach is to improve on that natural technique, even if it does conflict with the manual. But the failure to do this has ruined, I maintain, a great many cricketers.

People are afraid to encourage the hook shot. But it's one of the vital bits of armour for the early order batsman. If you are going to let a bowler frighten you with his bouncer, you aren't doing your job. Once you've mastered the art of hooking, you won't get so many bouncers. It doesn't matter how many you face if you're in the right place.

I can't remember Herbert Sutcliffe, George Gunn, Eddie Paynter, Patsy Hendren and Les Ames ever letting a bouncer go by. It's a gift. But you must have a feeling of absolute mastery.

As he watched the Test matches on his television set at Verwood, Gimblett despaired of players who could not hook properly. He was equally impatient with cricketers who ducked at balls which, as he said, were going six inches over the stumps.

Rough justice on Robins

Cricket again after the war. There was the smell of fresh paint – and eternal optimism – at the county ground in Taunton.

The nucleus of trusties had returned: to make the same jokes and shuffle the cards with the same dexterity. Some of them had discernibly aged. Wellard's nut-brown face had a few more creases. The classical 12 o'clock bowling action of Andrews was, perhaps, now just two or three minutes to the hour!

The war had coloured their attitudes. They were a trifle more militant, though eminently good-natured for most of the time. They had grown up and, like many of the pros around the country, were less subservient. Labour was in at the polls and the last remnants of feudalism would soon be gone for ever. Cricket, as a microcosm of the social order, was also on the march. All those initials, fancy caps and separatism were almost obsolete.

E. F. (Bunty) Longrigg remained the captain for the 1946 season. He was a Bath lawyer, a sleek-haired short leg who handled his bowlers intelligently and was worth his place as a left-hand bat. Bunty found himself with a fine team, even if in one or two cases the legs were not quite so willing. Somerset finished in fourth position, the highest they had been for well over half a century. In one marvellous spell over sixteen matches, from 22nd June, the county remained unbeaten. More than that, there were twelve victories: Cambridge University, Hampshire, Middlesex, India, Kent and Surrey were defeated by an innings.

To diehards, weaned on Somerset's humble status, the 1946 form was a staggering revelation. M.C.C. members, wedged in the leather chairs of their London clubs, squinted incredulously at the championship table in *The Times* as if they were victims of an optical illusion.

Somerset's triumph was also Gimblett's. He scored seven centuries, including the first double-century of his career. His aggregate was 1,947 runs and his average just under 50.

Physically he, too, had aged. He was no longer the boy from Bicknoller. He looked rather stockier, more mature. The blitzes on Plymouth and Bristol had left their mark. His batting style also showed a subtle change. The boyish flashing of the Athelney willow was less evident. The technique illustrated refinement. Blissfully, the exhilarating muscle was still there.

He harboured his hint of animosity for R. W. V. Robins because of a so-called slight before the war. When they met again, nothing was said but Gimblett was especially vicious with the straight drive. 'I heard Leslie Compton behind the stumps wince once or twice as I belted the ball back towards Robins. But he did get me in the Taunton match during July. I had no real complaints . . . ct Robertson b Robins 231.'

100

It was my first double century and on a beautiful day, in front of a packed house. And at the exact moment when the ball was on its way to the boundary for my 200, the bells of nearby St James Church rang out. It was a magnificent sound – and the timing was perfect, though I realized the ringers hadn't been looking out of the belfry to determine when they should start. The bells added to the wonderful feeling. I looked at the scoreboard and, very emotionally, thought: 'Have I really done that? Did I do it myself or was there someone guiding me? It wasn't the only time I had that odd feeling. I wasn't really a churchgoer at the time . . . but, I can't explain it easily.

It was possibly Gimblett's happiest season. He scored a fine century against the Indians in a match which I watched from start to finish. I came up with my sandwich box each day from Hendford Halt. I was there, on the first day, in time to see Buse and Andrews – in borrowed boots – bowl out India before lunch. I was still around, in heady ecstasy, when Somerset had won by an innings.

There was no train, sadly, along the single-track line from Hendford Halt to Bristol; so I missed the stirring August match that immediately followed against Gloucestershire. Gimblett made 133 but I am more intrigued by his memory of Hammond.

This was virtually the last time I saw him bat, just before he went off to Australia. There must have been 18,000 people in the Bristol ground. It was a wonderful sight. Gloucestershire won the toss and I think we got Charlie (Barnett) out pretty cheaply. In came Wally. Opponents were apt to be overawed in his presence. He never said much once he was at the wicket.

On this occasion he arrived in the middle and said, 'I must apologize, gentlemen. I've got a very heavy bet on a double century in this match and I intend to collect.' His bat got wider and wider. He went on to score 214 – and I never discovered how much he collected.

He was the most complete cricketer of my era. He could

101

make runs on any type of wicket. How can I forget the story I heard from the Gloucestershire boys about Tom Goddard's benefit against Notts in 1936. Things didn't look at first as though they were going too well and Tom feared the match would be over in two days. 'Don't worry,' said Wally. 'I'll make sure it goes all the way.' And he calmly scored 317.

Just once, at Bristol before the war, I was convinced we had them on toast. We had made a good score and then there was a thunderstorm. It was a very difficult wicket and we met with some early success. I can still see Hammond coming down the steps. Immaculate in his silk shirt. Blue handkerchief showing in his left-hand pocket. He looked like a prince.

He scored 160 not out. As far as I can remember there wasn't a single run behind the wicket. He didn't edge a ball.

Gimblett never hid his immense admiration for Hammond. He was grateful for the advice he was once given about how to play the spinners and googlie bowlers. At the same time, the Somerset man was conscious that he had exposed his deficiencies to the England captain. They rarely exchanged more than a few token words in the course of a match. Hammond was not enamoured of Gimblett's mannered air of indifference. He also considered that Gimblett's fielding, whether close-in or in the outfield, could be sloppy. It was a false impression, based on one or two unfortunate matches, and the seemingly lackadaisical demeanour of a man who pretended he could be spending his time more profitably than on a cricket field.

The 1947 season was less happy all round. Somerset stumbled down the table and he sensed that good friends like Lee and Andrews were on the point of leaving. There was less backbone to the side. Derbyshire's George Pope took 13 wickets to beat Somerset in a day at Chesterfield. New faces appeared in the county dressing room. Micky Walford turned up at Trent Bridge to figure in an opening stand of 209 with Gimblett. This school-master with the impressive pedigree could play very well indeed, he decided defensively.

Four centuries were scored by Somerset in 1948; they all came from Gimblett. 'Far too much responsibility fell upon him,' claimed Wisden. Lee had gone. The promising Hill, lean, stylish and anxious, often opened with him; so at some time or other during the summer did Miles Coope, Walford and even Stephenson, who had arrived from Durham as a brilliant successor to Luckes behind the stumps.

In mid August, Somerset went to Eastbourne. Gimblett was superficially friendly with 'that chap Walford' but observers noticed he was not forward in joining the general acclaim when the talented amateur had fashioned one of his attractive innings. It brought an added competitive edge to Gimblett's batting: so much so that he sniffed the sea breeze and scored 310. Micky Walford led the applause as weary Sussex fielders gave up the chase.

Do you know, I stayed on the field for 17 hours 50 minutes. I was then allowed ten minutes off by my captain to shower and change before I was needed back on the field. There was no possibility of a finish but he said we must declare for humanitarian reasons.

I'd passed Somerset's previous best score of 292 by Lionel Palairet, against Hampshire in 1896 but I don't suppose anyone on that Eastbourne ground realized the significance of my knock. I remember saying to Jim Langridge: 'Well, that's got rid of one amateur's name in our county record books.' I had become the first Somerset player to reach 300 and they couldn't take that away from me.

We went back to Taunton for the next match, home to Yorkshire. And this will give you some idea of the relationship between the club and its professionals – what they thought of us. Arthur Wellard went to see the secretary, Brigadier Lancaster. 'Harold's just made 300. Will you allow a collection around the ground for him?' The answer was prompt: 'He's paid to score 300. There will be no collection.'

I think that was when I first decided my career with Somerset was going to end. I was deeply hurt.

Such a notion, that he was ready to leave the county, was un-thinkable. In many ways he *was* Somerset. Even with the suggestion of restraint and caution that he had harnessed to his swinging bat, he was still one of the most exciting cricketers in the country. The fixture against Glamorgan at Swansea that same season made the point.

Everyone was certain that the wicket was going to assist the Glamorgan bowlers, especially Len Muncer, the off spinner. 'I decided that a little courage might induce the captain to take him off before too much damage was done,' Gimblett wrote later. The innings of 70 was dwarfed statistically by many others. But in his book, *Hit for Six*, Gerald Broadribb cites the Swansea knock as the Somerset man's greatest six-hitting feat.

Poor Muncer. He wrapped his fingers round the ball, pitched on a length and relied on the wicket to complete the *coup de grâce*. Gimblett, untroubled by a stratagem of theoretical perfection, attacked mercilessly off the front foot. Muncer, doing everything right, conceded six sixes in 13 balls. All the shots were straight and fierce. As Mr Broadribb recalled, the final eight scoring strokes were 6–6–4–6–6–6–6–2. It was a collector's piece for St Helen's, a ground that over the years has echoed to the sound of prodigious swipes.

Whatever his private thoughts and simmering sense of grievance, Gimblett was thankfully still around in 1949. For the first time he hit two centuries in a match, at home to Hampshire; his aggregate of 2,020 runs was a new county record. To reassure unsubtle supporters, who feared that his additional discrimination at the crease might devalue his natural fury, he impishly scampered to 40 out of 49 against the New Zealanders, and 52 out of the first 57 at Trent Bridge.

The West Country had long since given up hope of a Test recall for him. The selectors had forgotten all about him: their memories did not go back to 1939. They still erroneously thought of him as the young, hot-headed village cricketer, more adept at hitting sixes than dispensing social graces. Well yes, he had refined his technique and shored up that vulnerable defence, but he still made intrepid shots that you did not expect – or really want – from an England batsman.

When the West Indians came to Taunton at the end of May, Gimblett turned in an exquisite little innings of 77. There were eleven controlled boundaries and he was sixth out. Ten days later he made a masterful 184 against Kent.

Somerset's cricketing public, lovingly loyal to their neglected opening batsman, accused the Test selectors of being blinkered and prejudiced. No one after Jack White's time had the remotest chance of being considered if he came from a county as un-fashionable as Somerset. It was an insult that mocked logic.

And then, to everyone's surprise, the call came. Gimblett was in for the third Test at Trent Bridge. The argument, apparently, was that he could get after the West Indies' spinners. Every five-year-old in Hardington Mandeville could have told you that.

'I'm only in because Len Hutton's got a bad back,' the Somerset man informed his friends. The press took a more positive and romantic view; almost unanimously, the papers approved of his selection. But, of course, he did not play.

During the Warwickshire match at Taunton he developed a carbuncle on the back of his neck. Cricket's most headlined boil was treated in the local hospital and Gimblett rang Bob Wyatt, the chairman of selectors. Over the following days he was given huge doses of penicillin ('so much so that I temporarily lost the use of my leg') and travelled to Nottingham with Eric Hollies.

A nation's sporting press meticulously documented the carbuncle's throb-rate. He claimed that reporters cat-napped all along the corridor outside his hotel bedroom. Whenever he trotted to the lavatory, they shook themselves awake and asked: 'Will you be able to play, Harold?' He shrugged and gave them no news. The neck still ached. In any case, the head had been saying no for several days.

He returned to the West Country, through tearful Somerset streets; he took a few days off and then scored a pugnacious half-century against Hampshire.

105

When, in 1975, I was editing a Somerset brochure to com-
memorate their centenary, I asked Harold to nominate his finest
innings. He was forever a man of surprises. I knew Frome stood
no chance at all; but I imagined he might turn to Taunton
or Eastbourne. His choice was the match with Middlesex at
Weston-super-Mare in 1950. The Clarence Park regulars saw no
dazzling century from him – but a watchful, neat, technically
perfect 87 in trying conditions.

'I'm in no doubt that it was my best. The ball was going all ways.
Both Denis Compton and Bill Edrich said it was not only the best
they'd ever seen me play but that they frankly didn't think I had
that quality. It was praise indeed from these two great cricketers.'

Some kind of additional recognition came with his selection for
the Commonwealth Tour to India in 1950–51. Les Ames was the
captain and it should have been a happy, relaxed break for
Gimblett. He played in all five unofficial Tests, opening the
batting with Laurie Fishlock and then Jack Ikin. His aggregate
was a reasonable 289 with an average of 32.11. At Nagpur, just
before Christmas, he attractively drove and hooked for a two-
hour century against Madhya Pradesh Governor's XI. Play was
suspended for a time after lunch because of the death of Sardar
Patel, the deputy Prime Minister.

I had to play in nearly all the matches. But it was a bad time for
me – I had no energy, no spark, no conversation. I became very
withdrawn. At first I wondered whether I'd picked up a bug.
But it was purely mental. I was sickened by the continual smell
of curry and lost the will to eat. I lost two stone in weight. I was
in another world. Fielding which I used to love became a bore. I
couldn't wait to get home. It was 103 degrees in Bombay – and
snow at London Airport. When I arrived in Taunton I was so
thin that friends hardly recognized me.

In his book *Championship Cricket 1962*, Trevor Bailey described
Gimblett as 'a veritable Colossus' in county cricket. He regretted
that there were not more international honours for him. 'Nobody

knows how Harold would have fared overseas, although I have a sneaking suspicion that he might have relished batting on some of those hard, fast pitches.'

It is a lovely and reasonable thought. But I come to the conclusion that Gimblett was temperamentally unsuited to touring. He was too far from home and those he needed to fortify and console him. He was not gregarious enough to enjoy the social itinerary. He was too much of a hypochondriac.

Yet in my dreams I still see Harold Gimblett revelling in the fast, true strips of Australia and the West Indies. They would have loved him for his fearless hooking in Bridgetown – and he would have silenced them in Sydney.

Trevor Bailey, a player with brain as well as 'barnacle', took a professional's attitude on to the field with him. He was not swayed by sentimental considerations. Hugh Watts, now a headmaster in Ludlow, reminded me of the day the Essex bowler aimed a beamer at Harold when he was on 99 at Clacton. 'I've never seen anyone hit the ground so fast in taking evasive action. The other Somerset players were rather angry and, when it was Trevor's turn to bat, Maurice Tremlett was brought on to bowl. He was the quickest we had at the time.'

The reprisal misfired. Bailey remained vertical as the Tremlett beamer whistled towards him. His eyes were sharp and he did not flinch at that somewhat unsubtle act of retaliation. He swivelled and heaved the ball round to the long-leg boundary. 'It wasn't tried again.'

Gimblett returned from India and entered the 1951 season, slimmer and more visibly careworn. After struggling for form, he took a complete rest from cricket in the July. The doctors told him: 'You're run down – you've been playing too much cricket.' It seems that the break helped: he came back and scored three centuries during August.

As senior pro, he feared no committee man. Their practical knowledge of cricket he openly questioned. The permutation of skippers left his head in a whirl. After the surrealist musical chairs of 1948, when there seemed to be more captains around the county ground than church towers, George Woodhouse, Stuart Rogers and Ben Brocklehurst were appointed in fairly quick succession. His opening partners also came at times, it appeared, on a rota system. Hill, Angell and Hugh Watts in 1951; Gerry Tordoff and Walford among the others in 1952.

Somerset, the lofty grandeur of 1946 behind them, were just about to prop up the whole championship table for four years.

It was Gimblett's benefit year in 1952. He advertised his handsome wares with a timely flourish. He completed 20,000 runs for Somerset and for a second time topped 2,000 runs in a season. There was a century in each innings against Derbyshire; he failed by five runs to do the same at Worcester.

I'd hoped to be given the Gloucestershire match for my benefit but was told the county couldn't afford that. Morlands came to my rescue and I had the Northamptonshire fixture on their ground at Glastonbury. Morlands organized an excellent raffle which brought in nearly £500 – and thank goodness they did. In those days the beneficiary had to defray all the expenses. We played for three full days but my net profit from the match itself was between . . . £7 and £8!

The Glastonbury fixture, now sadly discontinued, was famous for its strawberry teas and hospitality at the mellow George and Pilgrim just round the corner from the ground. Boundary support was always wholesome and vocal. They still talk in central Somerset of all the fine cricket in that benefit match. Freddie Brown began by demoralizing the home batsmen with some marvellous seam bowling which earned him 7–33. Somerset had a deficit of 167 on the first innings – and then went on to make 413–6 declared in the second. Gimblett scored a glorious 104, backed by a remarkably fluent hundred from the blond and sunny Rogers. The only disappointment – apart from the beneficiary's balance sheet – was that such an absorbing game ended in a draw.

At the end of the season, he acted on an invitation and took his family to Rhodesia, as it was, for a six-month holiday. There was the chance of staying permanently but the pending political mood bothered him and, in any case, he had a Somerset contract to honour. He played some cricket out there and coached in two schools but he was ready, however grudgingly, to return for the 1953 season, a summer which reaped him another 1,900 runs and four centuries.

There were recurrent mutterings that he had completely lost his appetite for the game. Some believed the captaincy would be held out to him as a bait, to lift his spirits and rekindle his interest. Rumours were starting that he needed psychiatric treatment. Out in the field he looked preoccupied – though reliable enough still to hold 27 catches in 1953.

Gimblett recalled to me a broadcast by John Arlott when, commentating on Somerset's fielding, he is supposed to have said: 'And there's Harold Gimblett, studying eternity.' If John had only realized, he mused, what was going on inside the head.

I shall indelibly remember the 1953 season because of what happened at Bath. Earlier in the book I referred to Buse's one-day benefit match. In the next match, a fresh-faced boy called Langford did everything – and more – with his off spinners that Tattersall had already done. At this same mischievous Bath, Gimblett and Buse still managed to score centuries, and Tremlett was so seriously injured just above the eye when fielding that he never played again that whole summer.

At the age of 38 Gimblett was inclined to look an old man. He was still far and away Somerset's best batsman. The straight drive was as potent as ever; the cover was in Hammond's class. But, for reasons which came from within him, his career was almost over. I leave the words to him. They came out in a whisper, adding to their poignancy.

I couldn't take much more. I was taking sleeping pills to make me sleep and others to wake me up. By the end of 1953 the world was closing in on me. I couldn't offer any reason why and I don't think the medical profession knew, either. There were moments of the past season that I couldn't remember at all.

109

The Christmas was a complete blank to me. My doctor studied me and said: 'I think you ought to see the doctor in charge of Tone Vale' [mental hospital]. He in turn saw me at Musgrove Hospital in Taunton but I had a complete blackout from the moment I sat down in the waiting room until an hour later when my wife came in. The doctor turned to Rita and said: 'I think Harold had better come out with us for a few days.'

I was put on E.C.T. [electro-convulsant therapy] treatment. There were several of us having it twice a week. I felt like death but I remember joking to the others: 'Well, I open for Somerset so I may as well go first.' Rita came to see me and couldn't believe the difference. I had some colour back in my cheeks . . .

I stayed there for sixteen weeks and then it was spring again. Time for the nets once more. But I'd felt so safe at Tone Vale. No one could get at me. I just knew I wouldn't complete the next season. The first match was at Notts. I just folded up and had to stop the game while I was batting. I desperately tried to pull myself together. Reggie Simpson said: 'Go off, Harold.' I looked at Reggie and said: 'No, I mustn't. If I go off, I'll never come back again.' Of course, they didn't understand. I struggled to make 29. Back in the dressing room I was at the bottom of the pit . . .

He slumped on the bench and went into a bitter little monologue. 'I wanted to get it all out of the system in one go.' As a result of that outburst, he claimed, he was reported to the secretary for setting a bad example. Versions vary about what precisely happened during that match at Trent Bridge in early May and the one, immediately afterwards, against Yorkshire at Taunton.

Brocklehurst was starting his second year as captain. Like most others, he found Gimblett's moods unpredictable and disconcerting. He had gone out of his way to consult him, as the senior professional, in the previous season. 'Harold could be a delightful and helpful companion, and he made some shrewd suggestions.' Once he asked Gimblett which roller should be used between innings. The reply, given with a weary grin, was: 'This damn pitch has been rolled with heavy and light rollers for a great many years – and it won't make any difference which one is used now!'

There has been much vague talk about how Gimblett walked sullenly out of the ground after making a duck in the Yorkshire match.

I went out to the wicket and tried – I really tried. But I got caught off my gloves when Trueman was bowling. I came in and said I couldn't take any more. I was finished. It was my last game for Somerset. I knew I shouldn't have played. I packed my bags and went home. I moped about the house. Soon I was to return to hospital as a voluntary patient.

This is how Brocklehurst recalls it. 'Suddenly Harold was out, changed, packed and walking out of the ground with virtually three days' play still to go. The buzz had got round so I went to the press box and suggested that for Harold's sake, as well as the team's, nothing should be written for the moment. I hoped he would have recovered over the weekend and we could carry on as if nothing had happened. When it became clear that he wasn't coming back, I agreed with the secretary that we should ask him to come to the office. Only the three of us would be present. I pointed out to him that as the senior professional he obviously couldn't behave in that way. I suggested that after the match he should take a week or two off and then let us know if he was fit enough to continue. It was an unemotional and low-key meeting.' He went back to bat in the second innings.

In fact, he never played for the county again. For weeks he distanced himself from the county ground. He rarely checked the scores in the stop press. Now we come to a quite remarkable incident. I relate it again in Gimblett's own words.

Towards the end of the season the Indians were playing at Taunton. I suddenly thought I'd like to go and see some cricket. I self-consciously walked along St James Street with Rita. 'Nip up to the scorebox and ask Tom Tout if I can sit

111

with him.' Tom agreed and found a chair for me. I didn't want anyone to know I was there but it got around.

Tom went down to tea and he got the kitchen staff to bring me up a cup of tea and a bun. Believe it or not, they charged me. Soon after, I got a message that the secretary wanted to see me. I went down to his office . . . and he ordered me out of the ground. I was speechless. I just turned and went back to collect my wife. On the way I bumped into Ron Roberts, in those days a cricket writer covering Somerset. 'If you want a story, Ron, here's one for you. I've just been ordered out of the Somerset county ground.'

That had to be the final severance with the county I had joined in 1935. They even produced a story against me. It's possible that at some time I mentioned in conversation that I wished the club had shown more concern about my problems, more love even. I may have referred to the possibility of a cruise. The committee turned this round and let it be known publicly that the only condition I would play was if they sent me on a six-week cruise.

It was unthinkable that I could ever bat for Somerset again – despite efforts from Bill Andrews, R. J. O. Meyer and a few others. The county honoured my contract and I was then out of work. We had moved to Musgrove Manor, an old house with parkland and plenty of solitude. It was right for me. Or so I thought.

THE END OF THE INNINGS

Welsh connections

Out of work – and he panicked. For the first time in his married life there was no money coming into the house. And what, he asked himself, could he do apart from hit a cricket ball to distant corners of the ground . . . or milk a cow? He called at the N. F. U. headquarters in Taunton; there were no jobs suitable for him.

Gimblett was a proud man but he then motored to London and called on Billy Griffith at Lord's. The secretary was surprised to see him. 'We'd played against each other many times,' Gimblett told me, 'and it was actually Billy who was keeping wicket for Sussex when I scored my 310 at Eastbourne. As I passed 200, he encouraged me to keep going and try for 300.' The meeting at Lord's, however, was not exclusively for reminiscing. The Somerset man blurted out his story: might there be some sort of job within the game that Griffith could recommend? It was a friendly and helpful conversation, though he returned to Rita without too much hope of employment.

Confused, sick and angry, he had chosen to make himself redundant as a paid cricketer. He had made the decision without serious analysis of the alternatives.

Then he spotted a paragraph in the local paper, stating that Bill Andrews was giving up as the pro at Ebbw Vale C. C. Gimblett wrote off at once and a meeting was arranged. He explained the reasons for his break with Somerset. 'I want something that will help me to forget the past,' he told the cricket club secretary who also worked for the steel works. Hopefully to complement Gimblett's earnings as a cricket pro in South Wales, he was taken to the steel works next for an interview. The personnel officer noted Harold's experience as a fireman. Here would have been the solution but for a rigid shift system in the company which would have conflicted with Saturday afternoon matches for Ebbw Vale. In the end, it was agreed that he would have the responsibility for maintaining, inspecting and keeping an eye on all the fixed fire safety installations within the group in South Wales.

He liked the idea. Reluctantly he said he would join a union and would, as a short-term measure, put on some overalls and help out generally in the works.

Rita was not too enamoured, even less so when she discovered how draughty their hillside house at Ebbw Vale was to be. The atmosphere was very different from Taunton; Lawrence, their son, did not take to the new school.

Harold went home to sell, with some sadness, Musgrove Manor. He was just pulling away for the final time when he saw a cow about to give birth. 'I stopped the car to help the farmhand. We tugged and pulled. I'd done it all before, of course. I blew down the calf's throat. It coughed and spluttered – and the mother looked very happy. I washed my hands and away from Somerset we went.'

At the steel works, he clocked on at 8 a.m. He became assistant to a carpenter who was a rugby official and whose conversation centred more on scrummaging at the Arms Park than cricketing matters. There was absolutely no sign of the promised job for Gimblett. He was, however, whisked away to have his photograph taken for the house magazine. 'They had me in my brown boiler suit, wearing my county cap!'

During his time at Ebbw Vale, Gimblett met the local M.P., Nye Bevan, and was much influenced by him. For all that, Harold was a tardy union man. He joined the T.G.W.U. under some duress but claimed that he never paid political levies.

114

Life in the steel works was a strange experience for a man used to the open air. Some of the internal politics also came as a shock to him.

He was approached one day. 'You'll have to do an hour's overtime tonight.'

'But why? I don't want to.'

'It's the rule. We've negotiated it for you. You're in the Union, aren't you?'

Assistant carpenter Gimblett stayed for the extra hour. He did no work. No one, as far as he could see, did.

His version of what followed is equally odd, even if he strikes a few chords around the country. 'On the second week I was asked to do two hours' overtime. There was the same rigmarole. The union had negotiated it and I should simply take advantage. It seemed to me there were hundreds doing it. I suppose they were all on this lark. There was nothing to do. I spent much of the time between 5 and 7 p.m. wandering into the canteen and drinking tea.

'By the third week came the shattering news that I'd be staying right through the night. I just strolled around the works, had numerous cups of tea, tried sleeping on a chair. It was ridiculous. I let it be known that I was going home at 7 p.m. and not coming back till the morning. You just walked in with the gang, without touching the clock card. It was a racket – and it seemed to be going on all round the place.'

Gimblett got to know one man who drove a lorry by day and came in as a greaser at night. He had his corner where he curled up and went to sleep. It was generally known that he drew two wage packets.

Whatever the 'bonuses', this unhappily retired county cricketer was becoming restive. He decided the personnel officer disliked him and had no intention of giving him the job he had been promised. He told the cricket club secretary: 'If certain people take this attitude, I'm off. You can stick the five-year contract with the club up your jumper.' The secretary, sympathetic to Gimblett, suggested a word with the firm's doctor.

115

I was beginning to slide down the hill again and thinking 'Oh dear, here comes another one.' The doctor told me to take a few days off. I simply got in the car and went off on my own – I wasn't sure which way I was going. Somehow I ended up back in Somerset. I went to see my mother and drove over the Quantocks that I loved so much. I went back to Watchet and even took a look at the cricket ground there. But suddenly I was consumed with guilt. This was a fine thing, driving off from my family like this. I turned the car round and headed straight back for Ebbw Vale, arriving late at night. Next day I went to see a psychiatrist in South Wales. And he couldn't work out what was wrong with me, either . . .

Cricket started at Ebbw Vale and I had no enthusiasm at all. New friends wanted to see what I was like. The psychiatrist said: 'Give it a go – try to enjoy it.' Ebbw Vale were in the Welsh League but we started with a friendly against Brecon. I went out and made a century. Daft, wasn't it. I didn't want to play. The local papers got a bit excited and one of the nationals picked it up. 'Gimblett is at it again,' said the headline. How could they be expected to know?

Back at the steel works I said I was going to leave as the prospects weren't improving. 'Don't do that,' they said, 'we'll send you off to see the personnel officer for the whole group, in London.' And do you know who it was? Howard Marshall! The man I had known only by his radio voice. He begged me to stay.

Gimblett was given a transfer to the safety engineering department, a job for which he had absolutely no qualification. He continued making runs in the Welsh League but by the second season he had had enough of the steel works. His rural roots tempted him to glance idly at a copy of *Farmers Weekly*. He saw an advertisement for a second houseman on a farm near Abergavenny. With the minimum of formality or delay, he and Rita moved into a little cottage and he – on an impulsive whim – started looking after 72 cows.

116

They became my life for the next 12 months. I got up at a quarter to five for the milking. By 8 o'clock we had to get all the milk on board. It was a very long day and by 9 p.m. I was out on my feet. I went almost straight to bed.

But I can tell you I loved the cows. I developed the uncanny knack of being able to identify every one of them by glancing at their rear end. Daisy . . . Winalot . . . Eve . . . Peony . . . It may seem strange but cows were my salvation at that time.

It left him too tired to play in the mid-week competition that he had helped to launch at Ebbw Vale. The club, reasonably, pointed out that they felt it was part of his duty to turn up. He was prepared to continue with the coaching and allow the cricket club to alter the contract in their favour if he stayed away on Wednesdays. It was hardly an ideal arrangement for their professional. His days with the progressive Welsh club were over 'with mutual regret', as they say in the best circles.

He felt in need of a few days' break from farming. He took his wife and son to London. As he sat in Trafalgar Square, he read in the *Evening News* that Frank Edwards was retiring as head coach at Millfield School. In fact, the report was not accurate but Harold borrowed writing paper and an envelope from his wife's handbag.

'I'm sitting in Trafalgar Square,' he told Mr R. J. O. Meyer, his former Somerset skipper, 'and have just read of Frank's retirement. Have you thought of a successor? If not, would you consider me?'

By return came the Meyer letter: 'Dear Harold. We must talk. Wed, 2.30. Yours R.J.O.M.'

Gimblett kept the letter for years and was apt to quote it to civil servants who could communicate only in officialese and pompous mumbo-jumbo.

He reported to Millfield on the Wednesday. Jack Meyer's first question was: 'Do you want to play for Somerset again?'

For all his threats and public contempt for those who ran the club, Gimblett's reply was spontaneous. 'If they want me – and you'll release me.'

117

The rest of the informal interview was equally succinct. 'Tell me why you'd like to come to Millfield?'

'I have the feeling this is where I ought to be. I think I can help some boys in the nets. And I'm not afraid of hard work – I've been looking after a herd of cows.'

Meyer cut out superfluous areas of conversation. 'How much do you want?'

'Whatever you offer me.'

'I'll give you £10 a week.'

'I'll take it. Em – there is one snag . . . I've – I've got a son.'

'Where is he?'

'In the car.'

'Fetch him.'

Gimblett watched in silent admiration as the headmaster interviewed Lawrence on the spot. 'All right, I'll have your son as well. When can you start?'

And so Gimblett was leaving the little farm cottage and coming back to Somerset. The playing return with the county never materialized, of course. 'R. J. O. tried but ran up against a barrier. I'd supposedly upset, affronted, too many of the committee. It didn't really worry me. Bill Andrews also did his best at this time to get me back. There were too many unforgiving people. "Forget it!" I told my well wishers.'

Gimblett remained at Millfield for 20 years; the family home was now Barton St David. At the school he was to have various jobs. He helped to convert parkland into an excellent playing area at Kingweston; he drove the school van on the daily delivery rounds; he graduated to what he described as 'a kind of Clerk of the Works'; he ran the sports shop. He was happiest of all when assisting with the cricket coaching. There was a pastoral element to this. 'Boys would occasionally cry and tell me their personal problems.' They also doted on his words of advice when it came to batting.

He got on well with Frank Edwards, a fine slow bowler who played for Bucks. They had only one row; it was the coach's day off and, following a thunderstorm, Harold left the job he had been given to roll the wickets, a gesture of personal initiative that was not appreciated. He had, too, one or two minor reprimands from the headmaster. They did not dim Gimblett's considerable admiration for R.J.O.

'If he gave me a rocket and then realized it hadn't been my fault, he would send me a little reward. It might be a bottle of beer, until he realized I didn't like the stuff. Then a box of chocolates. Once he told me to take my wife out, buy her an Easter bonnet and charge it up to him. He was endearing and always unpredictable. They used to say he could charm the hairs off a gooseberry. And the progress of Millfield was a tribute to him.'

Gimblett loved the colour of the national costumes on parents' day. Like all the other staff, he had fun spotting film stars. He talked with John Mills and Stanley Baker. 'And they do say Elizabeth Taylor was once put in her place by Boss.'

After Edwards as coach came Sam Pothecary, the former Hampshire player, and then Gerry Wilson, who used to recall how as a lad on the Lord's scoreboard he had seen Gimblett cart Moss for a straight six off the opening ball. The Millfield bursar, Brigadier A. H. Mackie, in his crisp, military manner, had told Harold in the early days at the school: 'There won't be a dull moment here, I promise you.' And so it proved, under the idiosyncratic rule of Jack Meyer. After Brigadier Mackie came Mr R. W. B. (Dick) Redman, who became a confidant and friend of Gimblett.

There was to be no more cricket for Somerset – but plenty of matches for R.J.O. 'We played against South Oxford Amateurs and I was just about to go out to bat as the opener when R.J.O. suddenly said: "It's going to be too easy. Let's have a bit of fun. I'm going to reverse the order and put you in last, Harold." That struck me as a bit odd – especially when we had lost the first seven wickets for eight runs. He then promoted me from No 11 to 9. I made a hundred, R.J.O. got 40 odd and Gerry Wilson also did well. We topped 200!'

In time, Colin Atkinson took over as headmaster from Meyer. He, too, had captained Somerset, and is currently its president.

Gimblett meanwhile was being bothered increasingly by back trouble.

My relationship with Millfield gradually got edgy. I began to hate the place and the people there. Don't ask me why. I had a sense of failure again because I was told I wasn't making enough money at the sports shop. It all built up. The signs were familiar and I knew I had to get away from Street. I do apologize to Ellesmere College in Shropshire with whom I accepted a post. When I realized what I'd done, I knew I couldn't go through with it.

I can't explain the hate I now possessed. Millfield had given me so many good times. I'd helped to put ten boys, like Peter Denning, Phil Slocombe and Graham Burgess, into first class cricket – and that was very gratifying.

Things crowded in on me and I folded for a second time. I was given eight more electric-convulsant treatments. This time they didn't really help me at all. I was also limping badly and feeling in a thoroughly bad physical shape. Colin Atkinson said I could sit in a chair to do the coaching, if I wished. But I knew that would never work. I was proud of the technique I'd built up for winning boys' confidence in the nets.

Eventually, on medical advice, I decided to retire. I made sure it was done very quietly. I sold my house and moved to Minehead, though my first inclination was to get to the middle of Exmoor away from everything. In a beautiful old house at Minehead, not far from the centre of the town I was able to sit in a chair by the window and see parts of Exmoor and the Quantock hills. I had to accept that I'd never do any more physical work. I was on the scrapheap. My way of life, I knew, would have to change. I'd have to live on a tight budget.

I was cheered by a feeling of friendship around me at Minehead. My left leg was hurting badly when I walked. I asked a doctor for a frank opinion and he said: 'Your back is in a terrible mess from playing so much cricket. You've got a

120

trapped nerve in your left leg. That won't get any better. I want to take a cartilage out in your right leg.'

That seemed to ensure one sound leg at least. I had ten marvellous days in hospital. We were all cheering each other up. When I was being wheeled in for my op, I looked at the two porters in their grey uniforms. 'Umpires will be properly dressed at all times,' I joked. They entered into the spirit of the harmless little charade and returned in immaculate white coats. As I was just ebbing into unconsciousness, someone asked: 'Which guard would you like?'

That stay in hospital, in such a caring environment, caused me to do some thinking. I was grateful to the blind physiotherapist who did wonderful things. As I hobbled round on my sticks, I began to think I should do more for others – and I still do. If someone wants to get in touch with me, someone at the end of their tether . . . I've been twice through hell. I'm not ashamed to talk about it.

I end the chapter with a personal memory of Harold Gimblett's last game of cricket. In 1975 Somerset were celebrating their centenary. Bill Andrews wanted to arrange something for Clarence Park, the Weston-super-Mare ground where, as a boy, he had worked the scoreboard.

Bill had rustled up a wonderful eleven of former Somerset players to compete against a celebrity side. It was an afternoon of immeasurable joy in the sun and it was watched by a crowd of several thousand. Everyone wanted to play and as someone who had helped Bill with the organization, I earned myself an ecstatic, if dubious, inclusion in the so-called celebrity squad of 17 (fielders permutated).

Harold walked to the wicket at No. 1. The nostalgic warmth stretched out to him from every corner of the ground. He approached the stumps slowly and there were tears in his eyes. 'Give us a straight six,' shouted Arthur Wellard.

Everyone willed him to make a few runs. He looked nervous. David Allen, the former Gloucestershire off spinner magically transformed to new-ball specialist for the requirements of the day, tossed up a kindly half-volley. And Gimblett, the game's major attraction, hit it straight to me at short mid on.

My duty was plain. I stumbled and put down the catch. Hopefully it looked like an appalling lapse of fielding, from the boundary seats. Harold and I exchanged a furtive glance. It was a moment of rapport to cherish. I like to think it was the best thing I ever did on a cricket field.

THE EXPLANATIONS?

So many phobias

It is now time to gather up the bizarre, conflicting strands – in an effort to understand Harold a little better.

Throughout his perplexed adult life he was periodically burdened by phobias and various forms of paranoia. He catalogued what he saw as broken promises and rejection. Some of the festering complexes were still on his lips in the closing days of his life. He was unforgiving: for instance, he claimed that no one from the county went to visit him in hospital at Tone Vale, when he first went there for a course of E.C.T. That, he repeated years later, was especially hurtful to him. He came to hate officials and some committee members of the Somerset club, and the game of cricket as a whole. In the same way, he eventually came to hate Millfield School ('I can't say why, after they so kindly gave me a job'), pious churchmen who pontificated impersonally, politicians and property speculators. The hate – his uncompromising word – was spread over a wide area.

He worried incessantly about money when often there was no need. In his last cassette, recorded in a weak, faltering voice, he returns repeatedly to the theme of insecurity and fears about providing for his wife and himself in their old age.

During his playing career, other players were apt to notice a streak of meanness. One of them told me: 'As a light-hearted diversion, we introduced a scheme for levying a fine of a shilling when anyone in the Somerset party was caught taking a drink right-handed on a Monday. The twelfth man collected the fines and the money was used for our Saturday night beer-up. After just a week Harold complained that as he only had the occasional gin and tonic, while most of the others were mopping back pints, it wasn't fair to him and he opted out.'

Certainly during his benefit year he became rather obsessed with the way the money was coming in, though that from my experience was hardly a unique attitude. 'He would spend ages looking at the subscription list outside the pavilion and I saw him more than once go up to a well-heeled member and say pointedly that he felt the response so far was disappointing.'

With some of his benefit money he made a modest investment in a mushroom-growing enterprise and that was a failure. He had the cricket professional's outlook for getting the best possible contract. On one occasion he organised a round-robin in the dressing room. It met with limited support and he questioned the backing of his own teammates.

This brings us to his overriding sense of rejection. Although in truth he chose to leave Somerset, he was upset when the committee vetoed the comeback that R. J. O. Meyer and others were advocating. Eric Hill, by then on the committee, told me: 'The decision was made partly on medical advice but mainly because of the effect we felt failure might have on Harold and the team.' There were other incidents, including his apparent flop as a Taunton trialist and the brushes at Lord's, that he construed as abject rejection.

Gimblett was wooed back to the county sufficiently to serve on the executive for three years in the early Sixties. He was typically outspoken in his views and came out strongly for the policy of registering overseas players like Peter Wight, Colin McCool and Bill Alley. Then – apart from leisurely matches for Millfield and two seasons of enjoyable weekend cricket with Yeovil – he receded very much as a public figure before suddenly bouncing back in Somerset's 1975 centenary year.

He took everyone by surprise. On his own initiative he launched his 'Save Somerset' appeal. In a flurry of hitherto unknown enthusiasm for the county he began ringing newspapers with requests for publicity, and appearing on the television. His idea was for every cricket lover in Somerset to contribute just 50p. That, he calculated, would bring in £150,000. He would take charge of the money, invest it and, for the time being, not let anyone else get their hands on it. There were a few implied conditions. One or two committee members he saw as 'drones' would seemingly not be welcome to stay in office. In the official centenary publication, he wrote: 'My appeal was launched in anger. Here we had our special year and the club seemed to me to be dithering . . .'

Gimblett was moved to tears by some of the contributions, from schoolchildren and pensioners. But the overall response was a great disappointment. Only £5,000 was raised. 'I shall never forgive the people of Somerset. All I wanted from them was the cost of a couple of glasses of beer – and they let me down.' Eric Hill says: 'I'm sure the failure of this appeal was regarded by him as the final rejection by the public he had served with such distinction.'

Late in that 1975 season, Gimblett accepted an invitation from Bill Andrews to be the principal guest at the Weston-super-Mare (Somerset C.C.C.) area's centenary dinner. It was a convivial occasion, appropriately full of self-congratulations and without a note of controversy. The county's former batting idol was warmly applauded as he rose to speak. The assembled company sipped their liqueurs and leaned back in happy anticipation of gentle, anecdotal nostalgia. They should have known better than that.

The main speaker dispensed with the social preliminaries. He glared at his audience – and launched into them. He bitterly criticized them, as Somerset supporters, for their niggardly attitude towards his appeal; he lambasted the press for being tardy with their headlines over the same cause. It was a blistering speech all round and everyone began to fidget awkwardly. No one would accuse Gimblett ever of hypocrisy. Few would extol his tact. That evening in a large Weston-super-Mare hotel his cumulative bitterness went over the top.

Towards the end of his speech he changed key and came up with another surprise. He announced that he was planning a sponsored walk for himself: from John O'Groats to Lands End. He would walk for a penny a mile and he told his startled audience, rather arbitrarily, that he wanted 23,000 people to pledge their support.

Rita told me: 'On the way to the dinner he warned me of surprises when he got to his feet. He hadn't confided his intention of a marathon walk to me and I knew he wasn't fit enough.'

Harold said later: 'The mind boggled at what I could have made for the county and I could see myself walking through Somerset with a collecting can round my neck, shaking hands as I went. I'd have dearly loved to do it. But my doctor had other ideas. He said my back would never allow it – and that was that.'

As the dinner organizer, the crestfallen Andrews was very much to the point. 'It was the biggest let-down of my life. I could have had a dozen speakers but thought it would buck Harold up to ask him along. What he said was so unnecessary. It ruined my dinner. And, apart from that, he got all the headlines next day!'

We have discussed in the book Gimblett's difficulty in establishing many long-standing cordial relationships. He could too easily be openly hostile. It seems certain that he affronted Plum Warner on one occasion before the war; we cannot be sure whether that in any way prejudiced the Somerset player's Test prospects. I can only point out that Sir Pelham was warmly complimentary about Gimblett in his book *Cricket Between Two Wars*:

Some of his innings were conspicuous by the wide range of strokes and a certain uncommonness about his play which looked the forerunner of something akin to greatness . . .

In playful domestic mood, Rita nicknamed Harold 'Don' after the great Bradman. The Australian started out as Gimblett's

126

remote and revered hero; such idolatry noticeably lessened. 'Harold once tried to get me Bradman's autograph. The wicket keeper signed it in Bradman's name instead and that was a very big disappointment to both of us,' recalls Rita.

It was a slight, factual or imagined, to hoard with all the others. His relationship with God was for many years a tenuous one. In enforced retirement he was a devout Methodist and valued most of all friendships from within the Church. The welfare work he did, often in considerable pain, may have reflected his need to offset feelings of guilt about unformulated beliefs. Experience of death at close hand during his days in the Fire Service profoundly affected him.

There is some evidence that he relished controversy, maybe because of his condition, even needed it. He refused to suffer fools and was both impatient and angry with those who, with gossipy mischief, looked for additional flaws in his make-up. When he was living at Barton St David, someone said to a friend of his: 'What a shame Harold drank his way out of first class cricket.' It was an absurd notion, however much his dreamy demeanour and extremes of manner planted dark hints in the naive mind of a spectator.

Gimblett's behaviour, with its disconcertingly fluctuating moods, was for more than forty years a source of pain and puzzlement to others. He took many pills, consulted many doctors and maybe confided to too few friends.

Explanation of his mental condition is far from easy. Dr K. C. P. Smith, a consultant psychiatrist in the West Country, has had a great deal of experience in advising on the anxieties of professional sportsmen. In the Fifties and Sixties he was medical adviser for Gloucestershire C.C.C. Players, not infrequently, came to him to discuss everything from loss of form to insecurity. He found cricketers to be happiest when on the field; there was too much time left for them simply to sit and mope.

Much of Dr Smith's work in recent years has been concerned with the whole spectrum of personality disorders and he has developed the application of a new psychological Reversal Theory, offering fresh explanations for behaviour traits in various walks of life, including sport, the Arts and religion. His theory is that the subject has a tendency to treat life as a kind of game, in which he strives to reach feelings of high excitement or arousal. 'Any fall-off is felt as boredom. Some people find themselves constantly bored and frustrated and they describe this as being depressed. They often think the remedy is tablets.'

A low-key man like Gimblett, he said, needed high excitement. When he failed to reach it, he became phobic: hence talk of too much batting responsibility, ill health, money anxieties. 'He had strong "anti" feelings of aggression. He enjoyed hitting a ball around the ground, having revenge on the world at the same time. He could become enjoyably paranoid – as in the case of the M.C.C. – and play a new type of game against the establishment. But he couldn't keep it up, so became depressed again.'

I asked brother Dennis for an evaluation of Harold. The pair shared a physical resemblance as well as intimate home-truths. There was a mutual regard and genuine warmth, never more manifested than on the day Harold turned up, drawn and listless, at the Paulton vicarage, after the unhappy tour to India. Incidentally, he was earlier selected to tour that country in 1939–40 under Flight Lt. A. J. Holmes, in a party which included Arthur Wellard. It was just as well the war put paid to that. Gimblett could never really face India, however much he might be jollied along by his gregarious teammate.

Dennis had a great love for his brother who could be 'a kind and thoughtful man'. When Dennis was a prisoner of war in Germany, Harold went to enormous trouble to renew his brother's life insurance which had lapsed because of the war. He took it upon himself to visit an executive of the insurance company and personally to argue the case.

It cannot be easy for a brother to stand back and offer an objective view. They played orchard cricket together. They shared youthful apprehension – their digs were only a street apart – as Harold made his abortive attempt to work and live in London

128

'amid the oppressive bricks and mortar'. Years later, they philo-sophized about war, one a fireman and the other a PoW, and about God when Dennis turned to the Church.

'National fame was certainly not good for him. He always felt the pressure of it. Harold once told my wife that every time he went in to bat, he saw a great finger pointing at him as if it dared him to fail. In some odd way, I believe he enjoyed the spotlight of publicity but it could be a great burden to him at the same time.'

He was, said Dennis, a sensitive man. He blossomed when praised; he withered at adverse criticism. He was insecure and unsure of himself, especially when dealing with people. This caused him to become aggressive at times. Stress and strain were never far away.

Relatives and friends could seldom make up their minds about Harold's sense of religion. He voiced his misgivings about so many facets of organized worship. He veered towards the Free Church, and Methodist ministers and regular worshippers both at Minehead and Verwood were among his closest friends in the last years. At the same time, he remained a fraction detached from the activities of the Church. He preferred his religion to be on a more practical level.

'His religious life,' says Dennis, 'was emotionally-based and somewhat unstable. It was subject to his being the centre of its activity, rather than its being centred on God. He lacked the inner strength to resist the temptation to commit suicide. He was inclined to put himself first and God second. There was also a pantheistic streak which revealed itself in his love of natural beauty and belief in the divine presence of nature. From this, he drew peace and harmony. He was at heart a true countryman – he believed in God as the creator and not so much in God the redeemer. I have always thought his life would have been much happier and more full of contentment if he'd found a country job, out of the public eye.'

This brotherly assessment should not be considered a harsh or unfeeling one. It is an intelligent, perceptive man's view of some-one he loved and tried, like so many others, to understand. It is a statement of great honesty, devoid of domestic confection and the convenient sentimentality that goes with cherished nostalgia.

'Towards the end of his life, Harold retreated into something of a fantasy world. Day dreams became reality to him,' Dennis reflected. 'Things that didn't happen in his earlier years were spoken of as if they really occurred. It could be a little confusing to those of us who knew better. But it was part of the general deterioration – and there *was* deterioration over the last two years of his life. I don't think he realized that the suicide he planned for himself would adversely affect his reputation. In one way, I feel he thought it would give him one last great stance in the public eye – a kind of enormous hit for six, that would excite everybody's attention. It did so, but not in the way he mistakenly thought it would. Perhaps, in some strange way, he was the victim of a publicity he couldn't live without.'

Here indeed is a viewpoint that conflicts with what Harold would have had us believe, though it is substantially reinforced by the general conclusions of psychiatrists.

'In his later life, Harold always hoped to be recognized and pointed out, whether in the street, a restaurant or a shop. He liked people to dig a friend in the ribs and say "Look, there's Harold Gimblett". And in the end, it seems he just couldn't accept diminishing interest in himself by those he expected to recognize him.'

This is Harold Gimblett's melancholy story. It is now time again for his own words, because he insisted that they should be heard without literary confection. We eavesdrop at his request: he wanted people to know of his most intimate struggles in the hope that they would understand him better as a result. The words that follow were spoken shortly before his death. At times they are almost inaudible. Sentences taper away; at various points, they are almost unbearable in their ominous intensity. But they are his words.

I'm in a tunnel that has no end – and no light. There is no point in continuing to struggle against the odds. I came to this mobile home in Verwood because I thought it was a little haven tucked away. I was persuaded by glib words over the telephone and well-phrased advertisements . . .

The psychiatrists don't know what is wrong with me and there is nothing they can do in any case. Now I know what my father went through – I inherited it from him. The only thing I could do was play cricket and they threw me back into the first class game, after my earliest breakdown, before I was ready . . . I get more and more depressed. The only peace of mind is when I go to bed with a very heavy dose of tablets.

If I was on a life support machine I suppose one could switch off. I don't want to see anyone. I've nothing to live for. There's no point in going on. I can walk only with difficulty. We live very frugally. I'm 63 and can't get a job. And today I'm having a tremendous battle with myself. I wish 'Pan' would join me in a pact. It's a terrible . . . terrible day. There's a great black cloud sitting on me.

(Harold went on to ramble about the shortcomings of urban planning and high-rise flats, greedy landlords, his hatred of commercialism in professional sport, well-paid politicians and those pious members of society who did not consider anyone should have the right to take his own life.)

Maybe the coroner will listen to this and think what a load of rubbish it is. It is just a very unhappy, a very sad, a very disillusioned man saying out loud the thoughts that go round and round in his head. There is nothing I can do about it. Tomorrow will be the same as today. I'm – I'm becoming very emotional . . .

I'm a freak. Born one and always to be one. My father was lucky. He got a stroke which killed him at 55. Lawrence once asked his mother if I was mad. The short, simple answer is Yes – in some ways. There's a big weight pressing down on me . . . If I take tablets, it will be because I want to . . .

131

Towards the end of his final message he seemed momentarily to summon up added strength. He listed domestic matters that needed attention; he asked friends to keep the home warm for Rita and apologized that he had been hamfisted when trying to hang some insulating paper. He thanked the same friends for various kindnesses and asked them to keep a neighbourly eye on his wife. He requested from the Methodist minister a simple and private cremation, and a reading from Ecclesiastes.

THE EPILOGUE

Days with the Samaritans

Mrs Gimblett slept very late on the morning of 31st March, 1978. Her health was not good and she had not been sleeping well. On the previous evening she had neuralgia and Harold, even more solicitous than usual over her welfare, insisted that she take some sleeping tablets. She went to her bedroom just after 10 p.m. Harold looked in as he always did to give her a goodnight kiss; then she read the Bible and fell asleep.

She slept solidly for nearly fifteen hours. Shafts of sunlight were eluding the curtains. It was a beautiful day and Rita was shocked to discover it was one o'clock.

Their well-ordered mobile home was strangely quiet. Rita put on her slippers and went into the kitchen. She imagined Harold had gone for a walk and was surprised to discover that the back door was still locked. They slept in separate rooms and, still without any real anxiety, she looked into his bedrom. He was lying on his back, very peacefully, his glasses still on. One hand gripped the newspaper he had been reading the night before. The room was typically tidy; his shoes were perfectly aligned, as ever, under the bed. His wife rushed forward and shook him in despair. 'At the same time, I knew that he had gone.'

Rita remained in control of herself. Slowly she read the note that Harold had left, neatly folded under his watch. He had listed

133

the tablets he had taken. It was a formidable number and his wife realized that he must have stockpiled them deliberately. There was an empty bottle by the side of the bed.

Yet, despite his recurrent moods of deep depression and his abject sense of rejection, he had only once in his life discussed suicide with his wife. It was on one of the many occasions when he talked of what he saw as increasing ill health and hardship for the pair. He worried interminably about how they would eke out a living on their modest pensions and imagined how insufferable life would be when he was forced to sell the car. He had suddenly turned to his wife and suggested a suicide pact. Rita was embarrassed; she laughed uneasily and told him not to be so silly.

At the Bournemouth inquest on 11 April, a verdict of suicide while the balance of the mind was temporarily disturbed was recorded by the Deputy Coroner for East Dorset, Mr Nigel Neville-Jones. A consultant pathologist said death was due to an overdose of a combination of tuinal and amitryptaline. Post mortem tests showed that Harold had taken an abnormally high level of the drugs.

The Deputy Coroner described the death as 'exceedingly tragic'. He paused to mention Harold's long and distinguished playing career and said his fame was nationwide. He added: 'Clearly he was suffering from great pain due to arthritis in his legs and, having been such an agile person, I am certain that this worried him considerably.' It was a compassionate explanation but told only half the story.

Mrs Gimblett told the inquest that while living at Minehead, her husband had gone to hospital for various leg operations. After that, he walked with crutches or a stick and could not manage the stairs. They moved to the one-level of their mobile home at Verwood but he continued to suffer considerably from arthritic pain in his legs and this contributed to his depression. The Deputy Coroner, maybe a cricketing man himself, asked whether towards the end of his career, Mr Gimblett had become upset because he was expected to make big scores and found it difficult to do so. Mrs Gimblett said there were times when he seemed to have no support.

Rita returned to her Verwood home to look again at the cricket scrapbooks and faded photographs. She reflected again on that move to Verwood from their native West Somerset. It had been impetuous and ill-advised. Harold needed his roots, however much in the last few years he had denigrated the county which nurtured and acclaimed him.

Minehead was theoretically ideal for him. He occasionally rang me from there and rhapsodized about the landscape he knew so well, sweeping away to heather-clad Exmoor. He had good friends in the Methodist Church, like the Rev Stanley Withers. He used to lean on his stick and hobble along the aisle to take the collection at Sunday service. But at the same time he appeared to seek increasing anonymity. When people in the Minehead streets recognized him and cheerfully tried to draw him into conversation about Somerset cricket's colourful and variegated history, he recoiled. Once or twice, old-timers of good nature, more endowed with nostalgic enthusiasm than sensitivity, shook him by the hand and said, in effect: 'Hard to think of you hitting those sixes, Harold.' Then they would point, not intending to be unkind, at his stick. Such encounters made him angry. His brusque response could be misinterpreted. 'Old Gimblett's getting a funny bloke,' they would say. 'He can't take a compliment any longer.' What a pity they did not understand him better.

All the time, Harold was becoming more reclusive. He silently tended the flower garden and collected stones for the rockery. He sustained a talent for interior decorating and other modest facets of do-it-yourself. When he was feeling introspective, he talked into his cassette microphone. Apart from Robertson-Glasgow, he now had little time for cricket books. Cricket commentators on television were inclined to irritate him.

He remained restless. Once he contemplated moving to a cottage in an isolated corner of Exmoor but he knew that would have been unfair to his more gregarious wife. Lawrence, their

135

son, was employed then on the Isle of Wight and when they motored to Lymington, for the crossing to see him, they passed through Verwood. Harold had read about the mobile homes and, in a romantic way, they appealed to him. It would be a new, independent life, a long way from Somerset. No one would know him; no one would force him to reminisce about the game he now believed he despised.

The process of selling-up at Minehead was done in almost indecent haste. Rita says she used to retrieve little possessions when Harold was not looking.

They arrived at their new caravan estate home with fewer personal belongings and, to start with, no friends. In a letter to a West Country friend, Harold said he found the place 'quaint and friendly'. Yet they both knew, without needing to say so, that it was a mistake.

There was, however, much they liked about the village. They became enthusiastically involved with the activities of the Methodist Church, although by now Harold was not able to kneel when he took communion. He knew the words of many of the sankeys off by heart and sang heartily and often rather badly out of tune. He concerned himself with the welfare of old people in the parish. Rita and himself liked to take strolling walks, arm in arm, pausing to admire the front garden laurel hedges and kaleidoscopic flower beds. In Dewlands Park itself, he felt more wedged-in than he expected; all the same, he tried to give it some rural charm and individuality. He was proud of the camellia shrub in the middle of the lawn and that solitary, graceful poplar. Again he set to work to fashion a little rockery.

He got on well with the minister, the Rev Derek Chapman. They had many discussions, more philosophical than sporting. Harold would question aspects of accepted theology. He had long ago become disenchanted with what he saw as the rigidity of that Anglican faith which had first embraced him and which he once audaciously explored on a Bicknoller hillside with Archbishop Temple. He was now happier with Free Church thinking and the words of Wesley.

136

Mr Chapman found him very serious and deep-thinking. 'He never accepted things as they were. We often had words and I let Harold dictate the conversation. It very seldom had anything to do with cricket. He made it clear that he didn't consider cricket the most important thing in life and it irritated him when some people seemed to get it out of proportion. He didn't try to conceal his anguish. I got the definite impression, even from what was unsaid, that responsibilities weighed heavily on his shoulders during his playing days – and that too much was expected of him.'

His involvement with the Samaritans offered some kind of spiritual fulfilment; at the same time, the counselling stoked his own mental agony. He found himself repeatedly talking to others with suicidal tendencies, less evident than his own. Once a chirpy, even garrulous batsman, he was now the listener. The advice he gave, when asked, in that slow, morose voice of his, was invariably sound. But mainly his Samaritan role was that of a listener. He listened to dejected lovers and wretchedly lonely pensioners; to the physically and mentally sick; to the human derelicts. Then he motored home from the Bournemouth headquarters to live again the introverted agony of all those people who had cried for help. The experience exhausted him. He would lie awake at night, quietly weeping to himself. Only a short time before he died, he walked into Rita's bedroom one night and said of one young woman who had phoned him at the Samaritans: 'It's such a dreadful tragedy. She has everything to live for . . . a home, lovely children. I'm trying so hard, with all my strength, to will her into staying alive.'

Mrs Gimblett revealed a trace of understandable bitterness, maybe, when she reflected aloud to me: 'He suffered so much himself and he knew the desperate need for help and kindness. That painful interview with the young woman took so much out of him. In fact, her husband returned to her and the children and she went on living. But Harold died . . .'

The long relationship between Harold and Rita was a gentle, subdued, almost child-like one. They slept in separate bedrooms

137

for health reasons but they continued to kiss and cuddle, even in the late years, as if they were still courting. They had their own pet names for each other. Rita was 'Pan' (she isn't quite sure why) and Harold was 'Don' because, we suspect, she idolizingly likened him to the great Bradman. Mrs Gimblett was a child pianist who at the age of eight was performing in village-hall concerts. They both had social aspirations, with more than a hint or two of transparent snobbery. Occasionally they got on each other's nerves, like many other couples. Harold was a pessimist by nature; he agonized aloud and then there were domestic tensions.

Yet in the last few years of their life they were as close as they had ever been. Their walks around Verwood, on the good days, had a serenity about them. Harold could be effusive in his compliments over Rita's appearance. At times he implied that they would return to Somerset, as if momentarily consumed with guilt over the way he had impulsively left Minehead. It was an affectionate marriage. 'There are some things I shall never understand about Harold. And I shall never comprehend, however tormented he was, why he took his life.'

His deteriorating state of mind was apparent – at least in retrospect – in the final months of his life. He was highly critical of mobile homes in general. He wrote copious letters of complaint. He cited Members of Parliament for their incompetence and their sacrificing of integrity, as he saw it, for expediency. He ranted about the government for its lack of compassion towards the elderly. His anxieties about personal resources took on a bitter obsession.

Always an articulate man, he began to express himself less fluently. The handwriting was not so assertive. His cassettes, covering the closing days of his life, reflect a meandering personality. The voice droned on, soporific at times from the drugs if not despair. There was less logic; and positive paranoia instead when it came to tirades against avaricious landlords or unfeeling politicians. The disaffection with so much of life was all-consuming. No longer was there a trace of humour.

Correspondence to old and valued friends in Somerset had for some time revealed compounded anger, resentment and hopelessness. The preoccupation with material matters remained a common theme. To Roy Dight, a Taunton electrician who seemed on the point of finding the Gimbletts a home back on the edge of the Quantocks, he wrote: 'To move out of here would involve me in a considerable loss ... There seems no point in old age ... This is called an affluent society. I can stretch the elastic only so far. After that, away goes the car and if no one brings our daily needs, we shall starve. I once believed in our system of living but not now. So sorry to blast off like this but the last thing I want to do is scrounge off you.' In one phone call to this friend, Harold blurted out: 'I'm going towards a breakdown, the same as I had when I was playing.' He then broke down and cried.

A memorial service for Harold Gimblett, Somerset and England Cricketer, was held at St James Church, Taunton on 27 May, 1978. It was arranged by the Somerset Wyverns (the county exiles) on behalf of the county club.

When the idea was first put to Mrs Gimblett she had some reservations. She wanted nothing ostentatious. She need have had no worries: the service was cheerful, informal and religious. Harold, who liked his religion simple, would have approved.

The churchyard almost backs on to the boundary of the Taunton ground and the muscular young farmer's boy was soon, in the Thirties, demonstrating a penchant for landing his sixes among the tombstones. A match was in progress during the memorial service. Many of the congregation, still in their shirtsleeves, came straight to the church from the ground. We could hear, so appositely, the ripples of applause for Richards' boundaries, between the verses of the hymns.

The Vicar of St James, the Rev David Saville, conducted the service and the Bishop of Taunton gave the blessing. Harold's sister-in-law, Mrs Barbara Gimblett, played the organ. John Arlott and Brian Langford, a former Somerset captain, read the lessons. The pews were filled: with famous sportsmen and unknown supporters. Many of Harold's contemporaries, still with faces bronzed from many summers patrolling the outfield, were there. They wore their black ties and expressions glazed with warm nostalgia.

During his admirable tribute, Alan Gibson, cricket writer for *The Times* and a former Test match commentator, apologized for becoming personal.

Fifteen years ago I was in a mental hospital after failing to kill myself. Many friends wrote to me, sympathizing at that difficult time. The most understanding letter and the wisest advice came from Harold. As a result of that, we would sometimes in later years talk, not morbidly, about the problems of people such as us, beset by bouts of depression, often quite irrational. Experience of mental illness, he insisted, should be used to help others. He worked in recent years for the Samaritans and I'm sure he did it very well. He was concerned with many social problems, especially with the care of the old and the lonely. I was told he had worked out 'a bold and imaginative' plan for increasing the effectiveness of the Methodist Homes for the Aged. If you want a picture of him to carry in your mind, think of him first, not driving Larwood or Miller through the covers but chugging round Verwood, often in acute pain, taking old folk their hot lunches.

That indeed is how we should remember him: along with his first-over sixes, straight or over long leg, the bravado and the beauty of his stroke play.

Yet his stinging rancour and unabated anger cannot be ignored, just because of a cumulative imbalance in his viewpoint. Could there be anything more poignant than this sentence in almost the last letter he wrote before he died: 'I simply could not get on with Somerset or cricket any more.'

In the last summer of his life a doctor friend took him to the Benson and Hedges final at Lord's. Harold was in buoyant form and full of romantic notions about the game. The sun shone on him; it was one of his good days. But a single incident suddenly sent him plummeting back to his blackest mood of despair. A few days later he wrote: 'It was the final nail . . . I so wanted just to stand in the Long Room but was refused entrance. It hurt to think I had played for England 41 years ago at Lord's and yet this was the attitude of those puffed-up buffoons who wear those tomato-and-egg ties . . .'

He returns to the incident in one of his final cassettes to me.

I played three times for my country and was chosen a fourth time. I represented my country in the Great Victory Test. Yet I'm unable to enter Lord's unless I pay at the gate. If I pay, I can't get into the pavilion unless someone signs me in. It leaves a very nasty taste. It's a pinprick that festers from time to time.

The Lord's snub was not a deliberate one, of course. It was the System, inflexible and fatuously insensitive, that stood in his way. Gimblett, of the polished voice, son, as seen by some, of a gentleman farmer, was still the arch enemy of the Establishment and he blamed it for many of the rejections, real and imagined, that clouded his perplexed life.

We shall never fathom, even those of us who doted on his sublime flights of batsmanship, some of the sweeping contra-dictions in his make-up. He moaned more than most; he berated and he patronized. And a great deal of the time he despaired. His less engaging qualities can in the main be attributed to his com-plexes and tormented state of mind.

This is what matters. Harold Gimblett was the Somerset boy who engendered affection like no one before or since. He was a hero in the grand manner: yet the bravura never needed the flourish of the extrovert showman. He chose to leave Somerset in a quirk of unhappiness and was perhaps pining for home again in the days leading up to the taking of his life.

The demons in his head caused him finally to reject his native county and its cricket in one of professional sport's saddest human stories. For its part, Somerset and its warm-hearted cricket lovers will never reject him. He will be remembered with

141

undimmed affection. 'He brought pleasure and joy to so many. No one can deny that the game was enriched by the way he chose to play it,' says brother Dennis.

Harold Gimblett played for Somerset from 1935–1954

He scored 49 centuries for the county and one for the Commonwealth XI

His aggregate in first class cricket was 23,007 runs (av 36.17)

At Eastbourne in 1948 he scored 310 against Sussex

Twice he passed 2,000 runs in a season (1949 and 1952); he scored more than 1,000 runs twelve times

He gave immeasurable pleasure to cricket lovers around the country

He played just three times for England (he was chosen to tour India in 1939–40 but the series was cancelled because of the war)

He took his own life in March 1978

BIBLIOGRAPHY

E. W. Swanton *History of Cricket* Vol. 2 (1962)
Wisden Anthology – 1864–1900, edited by Benny Green (1979)
Sir Pelham Warner *Cricket Between the Two Wars* (1942)
R. C. Robertson-Glasgow *Cricket Prints – Some Batsmen & Bowlers*
  (1951)
Gerald Broadribb *Hit For A Six* (1960)
Trevor Bailey *Championship Cricket* (1961)
Ralph Barker *Ten Great Innings* (1964)

INDEX

146

147